Grim Phantasms

GARLAND STUDIES
IN NINETEENTH-CENTURY
AMERICAN LITERATURE
(VOL. 2)

GARLAND REFERENCE LIBRARY
OF THE HUMANITIES
(VOL. 1644)

Garland Studies in Nineteenth-Century
American Literature
(General Editor: Benjamin Fisher)

Grim Phantasms

Fear in Poe's Short Fiction

Michael L. Burduck

GARLAND PUBLISHING, INC. • NEW YORK & LONDON
1992

Library of Congress Cataloging-in-Publication Data

Burduck, Michael Lawrence, 1955–
    Grim phantasms : fear in Poe's short fiction / by Michael L. Burduck.
        p. cm. — (Garland studies in nineteenth-century American
literature ; vol. 2) (Garland reference library of the humanities ;
vol. 1644)
    Includes bibliographical references and index.
    ISBN 0–8153-0070-0 (alk. paper)
    1. Poe, Edgar Allan, 1809–1849—Fictional works. 2. Horror tales,
American—History and criticism. 3. Fear in literature. I. Title. II. Series.
III. Series: Garland reference library of the humanities ; vol. 1644.
PS2642.F43B87   1992
813'.3—dc20   92-19852
                                                               CIP

Printed on acid-free, 250-year-life paper
Manufactured in the United States of America

FOR S.E.
(wherever I may find her)

Contents

Series Editor's Preface

Edgar Allan Poe continues to attract readers eager to extrapolate from his works the "evidence" for his being a continuously intoxicated (from any variety of intoxicants) and intensely lust-prompted creature. The erroneous presumptions from such quarters, fortunately, are given the short shrift they deserve and speedily put to rest by Professor Michael L. Burduck in the following pages. Poe's preoccupation with Gothic horrors is well-known, although those horrors emanated less, if at all, from the author's personal mindset, but instead, and demonstrably, from popular culture in his day.

The present book is intended as an assessment of Poe's short stories that treat horror, and more specifically how he manipulated the conventions of that horror to register subtly on the fears and phobias of his reading audiences. As such, Burduck's aims succeed admirably. Using the primary texts themselves, along with a great amount of secondary material, over which he exercises evident and alert command, Burduck throws yet another cluster of illuminations onto the segment of Poe's work (the short stories) that continues to win accolades as his most significant contribution to literature. Thus the stories were designated by the late *doyen* of Poe studies, Thomas Ollive Mabbott, and his opinion has been borne out by the great bibliography pertinent to that body of Poe's output that has mounted for more than a decade. Although Burduck does not attempt to include within the compass of his book every story written by Poe, he does pay respects to what are probably the most familiar: "The Fall of the House of Usher," "Ligeia," "The Assignation," "The Masque of the Red Death," "The Pit and the Pendulum," "The Cask of Amontillado," "William Wilson," "The Tell-Tale Heart," "A Descent into the Maelström," "MS. Found in a Bottle," and "The Black Cat," as well as to a number of oft-neglected pieces, including "Shadow--A Parable," "Silence--A Fable," "Eleonora," "The Facts in the Case of M. Valdemar," and "The System of Doctor Tarr and Professor Fether." Such tales as these are unquestionably representative of Poe whole, so to speak.

Showing that fantasy is never too distant from reality, Burduck turns for support of his own thinking to Stephen King's ideas in *Danse Macabre* (1981) on the nature of horror as it plays on cultural anxieties, termed by him "phobic pressure points," and by Burduck "deeply rooted psychological and societal fears." Burduck reasonably ties King's ideas to expositions of psychological phenomena in the widely read medical books of Poe's own day, most notably those by Dr. Benjamin Rush, the famous Philadelphia physician whose name was practically an American household word in the earlier nineteenth century. Thence Burduck leads us on an inspiring tour into the territories of Poe's short fiction proper. He comments rightly that Poe's major exploitations of fear occur not in the ratiocinative tales (which for different reasons maintain a strong popular appeal) but in others such as "The Fall of the House of Usher," "The Masque of the Red Death," "The Assignation," "Morella," "William Wilson," "The Tell-Tale Heart," "Silence--A Fable," and "Shadow--A Parable," to name but a few. By means of close readings of the tales to reveal how "Poe used fear to build a nineteenth-century following," Burduck also argues sensibly for the continuing appeal of Poe's short fiction.

Burduck's book is straightforward in approach. The preface and first chapter set forth the author's intentions and furnish general background. Chapter Two focuses more directly on the theories of King and Rush. Chapter Three, the longest, is devoted to detailed assessments of Poe's works. Chapter Four furnishes a retrospect on Poe and fear, as well as placing the tales of fear within Poe's fictional corpus overall. An ample, if selective, bibliography follows. From Philip Pendleton Cooke to current Poe scholars is a long distance, but Burduck guides us along the pathway with ease. Repeatedly, he complements the work of J. Gerald Kennedy in *Poe, Death, and the Life of Writing*, as well as that of Joan Dayan in *Fables of the Mind*, both books published in 1987. His work dovetails, too, with that of Richard P. Benton, James W. Gargano, Kent Ljungquist, Burton R. Pollin, Donald B. Stauffer, G. R. Thompson, and others whose work is repeatedly consulted by those seeking knowledge of Poe and his writings. Burduck likewise contributes thought-provoking readings of Poe's tales, whether the much admired and be-criticized "The Fall of the House of Usher," "Liegia," "The Masque of the Red Death," or "The Cask of Amontillado" might be his quarry or whether the subject of the moment may entail "The System of Doctor Tarr and Professor Fether," "Silence--A Fable," "Eleonora," or "Hop-Frog," for which the bibliographies are not nearly so daunting--albeit that for the last-named is gathering prestige among Poe scholars.

The theme of live burial, a subject of recurrent interest to Poe's readers, admits of additional, and fresh, perspectives because of Burduck's critiques, as does that of vampirism. Matters of American economic and political import are also highlighted in a tale like "William Wilson," which, says Burduck, presents Poe's typical elitist protagonist from a new viewpoint. Burduck has also evidently learned well how to be heedful of the all-too-slippery boundaries over which horror and humor shift throughout the Poe canon. Thus he opens the analytic chapter by centering on that early Gothic work, "Metzenger-stein," along with several others from the same era in Poe's literary career, thoughtfully examining it for comic and frightening substance. Most appropriately, given the context of the present book, we are swiftly directed to the opening line in that tale of a haunted castle, its villainous master, and his supernatural horse: "Horror and fatality have been stalking abroad in all ages." This ill-favored pair of psychological tormentors have continued to stalk on with renewed vitality since Poe turned to experimenting in the horror story vein, and the outpouring of horror literature in which they flourish seems unlikely to diminish. All too often dismissed as a "mere" writer of horror fiction ("only that and nothing more," from his own "The Raven," epitomizes such long-continued ill regard), Poe languished while others from his age were brought forward as "major" or "representative" authors. The opinions offered throughout Burduck's book, however, may stand as persuasive testimony to the subsequent and ever increasing acclaim of Poe as a great literary artist.

Benjamin F. Fisher
University of Mississippi

Preface

About four years ago I overheard part of a conversation a colleague of mine was having with a student. I had just finished lecturing to my sophomore American Literature class, and I was walking briskly through the crowded hall and only managed to hear a few of my colleague's words: "Since Poe was a drug addict. . . ." Knowing that the professor involved, although no Poe scholar, was a competent, congenial teacher, I merely smiled and continued heading for my office without stopping to ask my associate if he had ever read Arthur Hobson Quinn. Normally I would have forgotten such an incident. As I unlocked my office door, however, I realized that Rufus Griswold was probably somewhere laughing.

Perhaps every Poe scholar has encountered professors and students who feel that only a drug-crazed madman could have produced the Gothic horrors usually evident in Poe's sketches. And perhaps, just perhaps, mind you, more than one Poe scholar from time to time has wondered whether the frightening conclusion of "Ligeia" or the bizarre masquerade in "Hop-Frog" was the product of a sound mind. Would a healthy, lucid imagination lead a writer to produce such "different" works? If the answer to this query is "yes," surely Poe must have had an interesting reason for portraying such odd incidents and unique characters. In other words, Poe surely followed a carefully conceived plan whenever he penned his horror fiction. What was Poe's plan? My attempt to answer this question led me to write this book.

Taking for granted that Poe was as sane as any other person living in nineteenth-century America, I began thinking about Poe's intentions. *Why* did he write these tales as he did? Students of American literature know that Poe valued poetry above all else in the literary world and considered himself first and foremost a poet. Yet he also took great care to produce short stories that would live up to his own high artistic standards. A meticulous craftsman, Poe strove for literary perfection whether he was composing a poem or creating a tale. Revision was almost a fetish for Poe, and he repeatedly fine-tuned his works. But what exactly was he working *toward* in his fiction? How did he hope to "hook" his potential audience? A popular twentieth-century author helped me answer these queries.

A decade ago I first read Stephen King's *Danse Macabre*. More recently I realized that King's book would help provide me with a clue regarding Poe's literary game plan. *Danse Macabre* discusses horror fiction and film and analyzes the intentions of writers and directors working in the horror genre. According to King, these artists rely a great deal on deeply rooted psychological and societal fears which he calls "phobic pressure points." Writers and film makers, then, consciously exploit the fears present in a particular society at a given point in history. Looking for the psychological weak points in an audience helps the artist achieve success. Giving readers or film-goers what they crave also insures that a writer or director will enjoy financial security as well. Certainly Poe, always concerned with making ends meet (although we must recall that he never debased his works by compromising his literary standards merely to make money), was anxious to develop a following for his fiction. Like King, Poe recognized the value of carefully analyzing current tastes and fears and producing works that would appeal to his readers. Poe's game plan, then, seemed to rely on the "phobic pressure points" present in the mid-nineteenth-century mind. In other words, Poe decided to use human fears to his own advantage, and his tales reflect the well wrought strategy of a writer who developed a very effective literary fear-formula.

Poe, however, did not have the luxury of looking into a crystal ball and seeing a copy of *Danse Macabre*. I realized that I had to discuss King's theory of phobic pressure points in light of some contemporary nineteenth-century theory. Was there a famous, popular nineteenth-century figure who discussed the nature of fear? This question led me to the works of Dr. Benjamin Rush.

A well-known man of science whose works dealt with many aspects of the medical profession, Rush published *Medical Inquiries and Observations upon the Diseases of the Mind* in 1812. One section of this book deals with the nature of fear and also lists specific fears that Rush observed in many of his patients. Such a work would provide Poe with the theories and observations of one of the century's most prominent physicians. Virtually all literate people living during Poe's time were familiar with Rush's notions, so it stands to reason that Poe knew the writings of Philadelphia's famous doctor.

Yet the scholar who assumes that Poe familiarized himself with Rush's works must proceed cautiously. Nowhere in his letters, stories, reviews, or essays does Poe mention Benjamin Rush by name. Thanks to the efforts of scholars such as David E.E. Sloane, David E. Whisnant, Carol Laverty, and Edward Hungerford, however, students of Poe can confidently state that Poe knew of some of the period's most significant medical writers. Sloane's scholarship in particular does a great deal to demonstrate Poe's knowledge of Benjamin Rush's theories. Whether it be Rush's comments on Philadelphia's yellow fever epidemic of 1793 or his remarks on dentistry, some of Poe's works appear, in part, to be shaped by Rush's ideas. No scholar has to date discussed Poe's fiction in light of Rush's theories on fear, however. Stephen King's concept of phobic pressure points and Benjamin Rush's medical views on fear led me to write this book, one which will hopefully provide new insights into Poe's artistic intentions.

Although Poe incorporated numerous Gothic elements into his poems and *The Narrative of Arthur Gordon Pym*, my book will focus on twenty-one of his short stories. Granted, Poe saw himself primarily as a poet dedicated to the "rhythmical creation of beauty," and many readers, years after they first encounter Poe's poems, recall the tintinnabulation of "The Bells" and the somber seaside setting of "Annabel Lee." Yet I find myself agreeing with Thomas Ollive Mabbott's opening remark in his introduction to Poe's tales in *The Collected Works of Edgar Allan Poe* (1978). Mabbott believes that Poe's short stories remain his major contribution to world literature. Popular during his lifetime, these tales are still eagerly read by modern readers, even college undergraduates who readily admit that although their perusal of "The Fall of the House of Usher" or "Ligeia" was forced upon them by a course syllabus, they enjoyed the experience. The lively discussions which have taken place over the past fourteen years in my classrooms make this fact clear to me. Even the normally silent students jump into the fray to give their views of Roderick Usher's secret or the motive for Montresor's revenge.

Today's readers enjoy the tightly woven plots and the precise style that serve as Poe's literary trademarks. The care Poe took to construct and revise his tales serves to remind us that he took great pride in his prose compositions and that he devoted as much time to them as he did to his poems. Of course, Poe's use of fear in his stories continues to ensnare readers as he forces them to face their own grim phantasms; his plan works as well now as it did almost one hundred fifty years ago.

I have selectively chosen twenty-one of Poe's short stories in order to examine how he uses nineteenth-century phobic pressure points to produce tales that will attract and captivate an audience. Some of the tales I did not include--his detective stories, for example--certainly play on the fears present in nineteenth-century readers. Admitting that my selection process was highly subjective, I decided to choose my personal favorites and, among other subjects, to examine just how I myself was "hooked." I will investigate the fears evident in "Metzengerstein," "MS. Found in a Bottle," "The Assignation," "Shadow--A Parable," "Silence--A Fable," "Berenice," "Morella," "Ligeia," "The Fall of the House of Usher," "William Wilson," "A Descent into the Maelström," "Eleonora," "The Masque of the Red Death," "The Pit and the Pendulum," "The Tell-Tale Heart," "The Black Cat," "The Premature Burial," "The System of Doctor Tarr and Professor Fether," "The Facts in the Case of M. Valdemar," "The Cask of Amontillado," and "Hop-Frog." A close reading of these tales, emphasizing how Poe used fear to build a nineteenth-century following, will also show why Poe's short stories continue to remain popular as we approach the twenty-first century.

After completing this study of Poe and fear I recalled the hallway conversation my colleague had with a student. Neither drugs nor insanity was responsible for Poe's Gothic tales. Poe relied on a carefully conceived literary game plan that was intended to capitalize on current public taste and the human reaction to fear. It seems that the last laugh belongs not to Rufus Griswold, but to Edgar Allan Poe.

Acknowledgements

I am indebted to the many people who helped make this book a reality. Benjamin Franklin Fisher IV, editor of Garland Studies in Nineteenth-Century American Literature, and Paula Ladenburg and Phyllis Korper of Garland Publishing, Inc. provided me with careful guidance and many helpful suggestions. My parents, John and Margaret, saw to it that I received the best possible education, and I shall never be able to repay them for their concern and love. Evans Harrington, Louis Dollarhide, and Ronald Schroeder of The University of Mississippi, Charles Sweet and Harold Blythe of Eastern Kentucky University, and George Cevasco of St. John's University all offered advice and encouragement. Special thanks are also due to the small but helpful group of people at Tennessee Technological University who assisted me, especially Kristy Light, "student worker extraordinaire," and Robert F. Bode of the Department of English, whose knowledge of computers proved invaluable.

Grim Phantasms

Chapter 1

Poe, Gothic Fiction, and Fear

POE AND THE NOTION OF FEAR

In "The Fall of the House of Usher," the narrator attempts to discover the source of Roderick Usher's unusual malady. Providing his friend with some pertinent details, Roderick reveals the true source of his illness:

> I have, indeed, no abhorrence of danger, except in its absolute effect--in terror. In this unnerved--in this pitiable condition--I feel that the period will sooner or later arrive when I must abandon life and reason together, in some struggle with the grim phantasm, FEAR.[1]

Fear plays a key role in Poe's tales. Most of the characters in the Gothic pieces find themselves slaves of this emotion. Skilled craftsman and artist as he is, Poe realizes that he must also lure his readers into a web of fear. His use of fear, then, must be directed at both artistically created figures and the readers who will either leave the book or remain spellbound by the story and follow it eagerly toward its conclusion. Poe relies on what Stephen King in *Danse Macabre* (1981) calls "phobic pressure points." Common to all members of a particular society, such points make them react to the horrors presented in a tale or novel. The good horror writer will exploit these inner fears as he strives to terrorize his readers. Attempting to reach as large an audience as possible, Poe decided to use the fears present in the nineteenth-century mind as the means of luring his readers into his fictive world.

How well did Poe succeed in grasping his readers with the embrace of fear? Perhaps the words of his contemporary Philip Pendleton Cooke demonstrate the effectiveness of his fear-ridden narratives. In a letter dated 4 August 1846 Cooke describes his reaction to one of Poe's tales, and he leaves little doubt as to its effect: "The 'Valdemar Case' I read . . . as I lay in a Turkey blind, muffled to the eyes in overcoats. . . . That story scared me in broad daylight, armed with a double-barrel Tryon Turkey gun. What would it have done at Midnight in some old ghostly countryhouse?"[2] Cooke later comments on some of Poe's other Gothic stories:

> I have always found some one remarkable thing in your stories to haunt me long after reading them. The *teeth* in Berenice--the changing eyes of Morella--the red & glaring crack in the House of Usher . . . the visible drops falling into the goblet in Ligeia, & c. & c.--there is always something of this sort to stick by the mind. . . .[3]

Although two years later Cooke would suggest that Poe's appeal might increase if he wrote about subjects nearer ordinary life,[4] his thoughts attest the power of fear present in Poe. No doubt other readers shared Cooke's views and found themselves terrified in broad daylight as they read a Poe tale.

The psychological machinations of human beings fascinated Poe: "he was always eager to arrive at exact analyses of qualities of mind."[5] Attempting to chart the hidden mazes of thought became for him a lifelong artistic quest. Of all the emotions produced by and affecting the mind, fear most intrigued Poe. Influenced by Burke, Poe knew that no other passion so effectively prevents the mind from acting or reasoning.[6] Like his narrator in "Usher," Poe sought to discover the true sources and nature of fear. Throughout his fiction he probed the mind in order better to understand this grim phantasm, which at one time or another holds every man in its grasp.

The events in his tales serve to reflect and heighten the mental condition being probed. Such external devices as weather and setting provide an environmental basis for fear. Poe highlights his description of mental or physical situations or moods with a concentration similar to that which one in everyday life observes in tense moments.[7] Understanding the mechanics of fear, Poe brings his knowledge of its characteristics to bear in the physical act of writing a tale.

Despite Poe's use of fear as a force capable of producing deadly results, many critics question his seriousness regarding this emotion. Lewis posits that although Poe's writings juxtapose terror and humor they rarely reject the power of fear.[8] Other scholars appear more skeptical regarding Poe's fiction of fear. In a famous essay T.S. Eliot questions Poe's sincerity arguing that Poe appeared to entertain ideas rather than believe in them.[9] To G.R. Thompson the irony used in the Gothic tales allows Poe to contemplate fear and yet detach himself from it as he spoofs fear literature.[10] Such viewpoints minimize the possibility of Poe taking his Gothic tales with anything but a grain of salt.[11]

Other critics comment unfavorably regarding Poe's fiction in general. Stoehr feels that "Poe's tales are . . . completely out of phase with everyday life."[12] Expressing a similar notion, Pattee remarks "nowhere [in Poe] is there realism. The characters are not alive. . . . We never see such people in real life."[13] When they do perceive something genuine in one of Poe's tales, certain readers immediately read the piece as a public confession of some sort of personal proclivity.[14]

Perhaps readers find Poe's tales difficult to believe because they often contain unusual characters or improbable events. Do these superficial features rule out the possibility of certain truths existing below the surface in the depths of the story? To answer this question adequately, one must be aware of Poe's ability to make the implausible or incredible appear realistic.[15] To those who view only the surface of the tales, these stories become unbelievable farces demonstrating Poe's ability to hoax or parody the excessive horrors used by other Gothic writers. Such an opinion fails to give Poe his due. Poe uses fear and other Gothic devices in virtually all of his stories. The tales of ratiocination, "The Gold-Bug," "The Murders in the Rue Morgue," "The Mystery of Marie Roget," "The Purloined Letter," and "Thou Art the Man!" contain numerous samples of Gothic horrors. In these tales, however, Poe focuses on the intuitive and analytical capabilities of the mind. He is concerned more with the mind's strengths than with its weaknesses. Like the detective stories, his satirical pieces, including "Loss of Breath," "How to Write a Blackwood Article," "Four Beasts in One," "The Man That Was Used Up," and "Some Words with a Mummy," feature elements indigenous to the Gothic tradition. Yet these tales do not attempt to terrify the reader. Poe intends to poke fun at currently popular phenomena or various political or literary figures. He uses not his ratiocinative or satirical tales but his horror fiction to explore the dark, ominous realm of fear. Horribly intense, the fear present in these sketches completely captures the reader's consciousness. The stories of horror are realistic because fear, their key element, makes the creations real. Fear is an innate emotion rooted deep in the mind. Along with love, hate, anger, and joy, fear resides in the depths of our being and often plays a crucial role in determining our beliefs and actions. By denying the existence of fear or shunning it, a person refuses to acknowledge what helps make him human. If fear is real, then those Poe tales dealing with this basic emotion center upon an important reality of existence. Despite the incredible trappings of Gothic fiction, devices which he certainly does use in his works, Poe addresses the nature of fear, the terror not of "Germany" (i.e. sleazy horrifics) but of the "soul," and its influence upon us. Poe's fiction of fear examines acutely man's mind and its manifestations.

Readers often categorize Poe's fear sketches as morbid. His concentration on such matters as bizarre death and torture leads some to doubt his sanity. Others consider Poe a literary pioneer. Commenting on Poe's stories, Foerster recognizes Poe's use "of ugly and harrowing things from which men automatically avert their eyes, of the strange functioning of the senses, the nerves, the subconscious self."[16] Foerster views the bizarre characteristics of Poe's stories as an artist's attempt to treat all of man's emotions. H.P. Lovecraft also praises Poe and his horror fiction:

> He saw clearly that all phases of life and thought are equally eligible as subject matter for the artist . . . and decided to be the interpreter of those powerful feelings and frequent happenings which attend pain rather than pleasure, decay rather than growth, terror rather than tranquility. . . . [17]

Realizing the power of pain, decay, and terror, Poe explored these feelings and attempted to enlighten the dark tunnels of human life. Like some of his contemporaries, Poe challenged the rather overly optimistic ideas formulated at the onset of the American Renaissance. Whereas certain of his literary colleagues would have shrunk back, Poe forged his way toward a better understanding of life and all of its aspects.[18] He attempted to bring his literary light into the depths of psychic darkness: "the monstrous seems to have led more significantly to a fictional discovery of the true depths of human nature than to a mere exploitation of the sensational and the perverse."[19] The depths of fear were not the least of Poe's concerns.

In the following pages I will investigate the fears present in some of Poe's short stories. My central concern will be the particular fears possessed by the nineteenth-century reader who ventured into Poe's world of Gothic horror. Through his acquaintance with such works as Benjamin Rush's *Medical Inquiries and Observations upon the Diseases of the Mind*, published in 1812, Poe familiarized himself with the fears recorded by the pioneers of modern American psychology.[20] Such early psychological treatises helped to shape Poe's perspectives regarding fear and madness. He learned what scared the nineteenth-century reader, and he consciously strummed those inner chords buried deep in his readers' minds.

SOME CHARACTERISTICS OF THE GOTHIC

Before examining Poe's strategy of fear, we should study briefly some of the pervasive qualities in Gothic tales. Scholars have spilled a great deal of critical ink discussing the tale of terror. Since Poe decided to use this genre as his chief means of relaying his artistic vision, a few comments concerning this form of fiction may help to clarify the relationship between Poe and the tradition with which he worked.

Originating with the publication in 1864 of Horace Walpole's *The Castle of Otranto*, Gothic fiction became a popular type of literature. Sinister castles, cruel villains, helpless victims, clanking chains, and supernatural visitors entranced the reading public. Writers of these tales were eager to explore new horizons in their works. Eighteenth-century literature had previously placed great emphasis on the mind's rational power. Order and reason reigned supreme. Many writers, consequently, produced works that adhered to a carefully planned Neo-classical formula. *The Castle of Otranto* helped to produce a counterforce against rigid Neo-classicism. Rejecting art that called attention to its own artifice, poets created works arising from the depths of the imagination. This new form of Romantic literature stressed the importance of emotion. Instead of imitating established conventions, writers would now admit the powers of emotion and seek to instill their works with an original imaginative quality shunned by more conservative literary figures.

Apart from allowing authors to examine new literary territory, how did the Gothic strike its intended audience? To many readers the term "Gothic" conveyed the idea of barbarism.[21] Some of the stock devices of Gothic fiction no doubt contributed to such a view. Despite the surface horrors evident in virtually all such tales, Gothicism appealed to some spiritual wellspring buried deep within each member of its audience. Critics realized that such fiction satisfied "the human desire to experience new emotions and sensations without actual danger."[22] Mussell speculates that such vicarious danger and Romantic fantasy appeal strongly to female readers.[23] Gothic fiction provides its audience with the sorts of adventures that help them to forget the dull trivialities of everyday life. The mundane falls victim to the fantastic. Gothic stories permit the members of the public to visit exotic lands and to meet mysterious people such as they would otherwise never encounter. The Gothic in this respect becomes a type of escape reading,[24] a form of entertainment which permits the reader's imagination to carry him into the author's fictive world.

Dark shapes exist in the Gothic world, however. Whoever ventures thither must prepare for the horrors lurking in the shadows. Although it owes its birth to the Romantic revolution, the Gothic challenges some principles of Romanticism: "the Gothic is the dark counterforce to optimistic Romanticism."[25] Whereas the Romantics seek to reconcile man with the elements of the universe, the Gothic writer realizes that such reconciliation often remains impossible. In America those great optimists the Transcendentalists were challenged by Poe, Hawthorne, and Melville.[26] These Gothicists knew that good does not always conquer evil. The struggle between God and

Satan rages eternally with no clear-cut victor emerging from the
fray. All too frequently, however, evil appears to gain the upper
hand. Gothicists dwell on the unpleasant, then, because the
sinister elements of existence seemingly rear their heads more
often than the pleasant aspects of life manifest themselves.

If Gothic fiction provides a means of escape for the reader,
into what sort of world does he find himself retreating? Coad
posits that the Gothic creates "an atmosphere of mystery and
terror by the use of supernatural or apparently supernatural
machinery, or of pronounced physical or mental horror."[27]
Viewed in this light, the Gothic attempts to subdue its reader
physically and emotionally by threatening body and mind.
Atmosphere plays an important function in the Gothic. A sense
of foreboding and intensity, therefore, pervades such fiction.[28]
Discussing the "weird tale," Lovecraft demonstrates the intensity
to which the author of Gothic fiction must force himself:

> There must be a hint, expressed with a seriousness and
> portentousness becoming its subject, of that most
> terrible conception of the human brain--a malign and
> particular suspension or defeat of those fixed laws of
> Nature which are our only safeguard against the assaults
> of chaos and the daemons of unplumbed space. (p. 15)

Lovecraft's remarks prove interesting because they express the
belief that the horror writer must view his work seriously if he
hopes to paralyze his reader with fear. Humor does little to coax
one into believing in the inversion of natural laws.

Earlier we saw how the Gothic tale works on both the
physical and mental levels. Gothic writers use tangible horrors
to subdue the reader's emotions and draw him farther into the
dark abyss of fear: "Horror is an experience of cruelty being
exerted fascinatingly and violently by a single personal force
upon a single personal victim."[29] As we shall see later in this
study, Poe uses fear as the force that assails the victim's body

and mind. Burke feels that physical and mental violence are closely related:

> The only difference between pain and terror, is, that things which cause pain operate on the mind, by the intervention of the body; whereas things that cause terror generally affect the bodily organs by the operation of the mind suggesting the danger. (p. 132)

The interaction of mind and body plays an important part in the reader's perception of fear, and Burke's remarks about terror help to demonstrate how the Gothic concerns itself with psychological and, often, sexual reality.

Two terms mentioned by Burke and Hallie have received considerable critical attention. "Terror" and "horror," despite their similarities, possess slightly different connotations when used in the study of Gothic fiction. In the opinion of Varma, the power of terror resides in the uncertainty and obscurity that accompany it. Not knowing what lurks behind the locked door terrifies the reader. Being unable to ascertain the source of anxiety places one in the realm of terror. Terror gives way to horror when the reader finally confronts whatever being or event lies at the heart of his fears: "the difference between terror and horror is the difference between the awful apprehension and sickening realization: between the smell of death and stumbling against a corpse."[30]

Other critics differentiate terror from horror, and almost all agree that horror's intensity exceeds that of terror. Thompson believes that terror strikes at the fear response relative to physical and mental pain but that horror suggests incredible evil or moral decay.[31] St. Armand likewise thinks that terror is an outside force attacking the reader's soul but that horror overtakes one from within.[32] Hume sees an important difference between the terror-Gothic and the horror-Gothic. The main factor determining the overall effect of these two forms of

Gothic fiction is the reader. Rejecting the external circumstances of the terror-Gothic, the reader simply closes the book and returns to his own world. The horror-Gothic, on the other hand, captures the reader by concentrating more on the fears lodged deep in the mind. If the events have psychological consistency and tap the well of the reader's mental fears, he will find himself involved beyond control.[33] The Gothic story relying on the internal machinations of the mind captures its audience by exploiting psychological fears. Resisting vampires or demons proves difficult, but certain protective measures do exist. Unfortunately no wreath of garlic or pentagram can protect the mind from itself. Although he uses some of the externally oriented trappings of the terror-Gothic, Poe directs himself more toward the horrors of the human mind. He prefers to scare his audience from within.

After the preceding brief summary of the Gothic and some of its key elements, we need to formulate a useful definition of this popular mode of fiction. In light of all the points discussed thus far the Gothic becomes an imaginative exercise rooted in psychological reality. Fictitious characters fall victim to the realistic human emotion of fear. By presenting such episodes the Gothic writer produces an anodyne which assists the reader in confronting life's stresses. Although fear persists and remains firmly embedded in the human psyche, the reader who faces it in fiction might also refuse to succumb when he encounters it in his own life. The thoughts of Varma support such an opinion when he states "the Gothic novelists touched the concealed, glorious, *intrinsically healthy* [my italics] primeval power that lay restlessly palpitating under the sophistication and form of the Augustan Age."[34] Terror and horror used properly in the Gothic might actually benefit the reading public. A reader could explore his own mental caverns as he perused a Gothic tale and learn something about himself. As an examination of his use of Gothic tradition reveals, Poe cleverly relies on his knowledge of the Gothic's true power.

POE'S STRATEGY OF FEAR

Poe acknowledges the power of fear and realizes that the Gothic tale provides a useful means of discussing this emotion. His use of Gothicism revolves strategically around his efforts to produce an extremely popular form of literature to attract readers. The tales must spellbind and capture the audience's complete attention. Popular taste becomes very important for Poe. In his fiction he strives to appeal to his contemporaries through the use of fear. Recognizing fear's alluring qualities, he entices the reader into entering not only the world of the particular tale but also the depths of his own consciousness.

Reviews concerning Poe's fiction reveal that despite an occasional unfavorable notice many critics found his work appealing.[35] Unable to achieve financial success, Poe managed to reach a good number of readers, thanks to the popular annuals, newspapers, and magazines. His contributions to these publications permitted him to evolve a variety of symbolist terror that has never been surpassed.[36] The public read these tales of terror and provided Poe with an opportunity to use his fear formula. Besides contributing fiction and poetry to various literary journals, Poe served as editor for a number of prominent nineteenth-century magazines. With the help of his friend John Pendleton Kennedy he became assistant editor for T.W. White's *Southern Literary Messenger*. Later he worked for other periodicals including *Burton's Gentleman's Magazine*, *Graham's Magazine*, and *The Broadway Journal*.

Magazines appealed to an audience possessing a wide range of literary interests. Articles appearing in these journals discussed such topics as domestic and foreign politics, religion, farming, sociology, and science. For the more literarily inclined members of the populace, the editors included fiction, poetry, essays, and literary criticism. Some of the popular periodicals of the 1830s, including the renowned *Blackwood's Magazine*, regularly featured tales using two motifs which intrigued the typical nineteenth-century reader: the adventure to exotic places and the death of a beautiful young lady. These themes figure significantly in much of Poe's fiction, and we can see the influence that popular fiction of the period played in the development of his stories.

Familiarity with the trends evident in magazine literature gave Poe valuable information regarding reading taste. He learned what sort of literature was popular and what type of fiction the public wanted. Concerned with maintaining a high literary tradition no less than with profit,[37] he would excite his reader's imagination with an art geared toward the audience's psychological response to it. No better type of literature to achieve this end existed than that which explored the nature and effects of fear.

Poe makes an interesting remark in his "Marginalia" in the June 1849 issue of the *Southern Literary Messenger*: "the nose of a mob is its imagination. By this, at any time, it can be quietly led."[38] Disliking the notion of a poorly educated "mob," Poe realizes that all people, even those not intelligent enough to appreciate the finer points of art, react when their imaginations are stimulated. A work that tempts the imagination automatically appeals to readers. Arousing readers' curiosity helps the writer to insure the popularity of his fiction. Through his work with the magazines of his day Poe possessed a firm knowledge of both popular taste and the functioning of the human mind.[39] Armed with such information he spearheaded an attack deep into the psychological realm of fear.

In all his Gothic fiction, Poe remains aware of the curious appeal of fear, terror, and horror. For some reason these elements attract readers. As Lovecraft remarks, "Poe so clearly and realistically understood the natural basis of the horror-appeal . . . " (p. 66). Knowing how readers readily devoured fiction featuring murder, torture, disease, and death, Poe incorporated these features into his tales. Various critics speculate on the reasons behind the attraction to fear.[40]

Edmund Burke provides a philosophical basis regarding fear and a person's desire to experience it. Poe seems to be aware of Burke's theories concerning this matter and uses these ideas as he creates his tales.

Commenting on the origins of the term "fear," Burke shows that the Latin *stupeo* means fear or astonishment (p. 58). On the basis of this revelation Poe and other readers could see the similarity between fear and wonder. A person may become terrified in a particular situation but still express wonder as he contemplates his predicament. Beauty exists side by side with terror and horror. Various spectacles in the natural world and, one must assume, mental perceptions as well, produce such experience. Burke speculates:

> Whatever is fitted in any sort to excite the ideas of pain and danger, that is to say, whatever is in any sort terrible, or is conversant about terrible objects or operates in a manner analogous to terror, is a source of the *sublime*; that is, it is productive of the strongest emotion which the mind is capable of feeling. (p. 39)

For Burke, then, the sublime elevates one's mind to the point where a person becomes attracted to the source of such stimulation. Some of the qualities that produce the sublime include obscurity, power, privation, vastness, infinity, difficulty, magnificence, and loudness. Later we shall see how these sources of the sublime relate to the fears described by Benjamin Rush.

Burke believes that pain and danger possess the ability to delight the mind. He uses the example of physical exercise to illustrate his point. The pain resulting from such action provides delight because it relieves the boredom of inactivity (pp. 134-135). Such pain also helps one develop a strong body. Along with physical activity, mental liveliness also benefits a person. The active, well-developed mind keeps one alert and permits one to face whatever mental challenges arise. One of the most intense problems the mind encounters is that presented by pain and fear. Both recognizing and facing this condition delight a person because he must exercise his mental faculties to conquer his misgivings.

Poe accepts Burke's theories regarding the production of the sublime. Faced with terror, the mind must grapple with the paradoxical responses of dread and desire. Burke, however, fails to describe such events as "pleasurable" because pain does not directly produce pleasure. Is there some legitimate way for terror to please a reader? Heller suggests that Poe relies on terror's ability to fill the reader with a feeling of satisfaction:

> The pleasure of reading a tale which to some degree attempts a direct attack of terror on the reader derives from the reader's successful exercise of his faculties of personal integration in resistance to the threats posed by the story.[41]

This concept presupposes that the writer can draw his reader from his own society into the "world" of the tale. Becoming a part of the author's fictive universe, the reader gratifies himself by enduring those fears that overcome the protagonists. By personalizing the story, the author makes his audience imaginatively experience the fear present in the work. Poe understands this process and attempts to capture his reader with it.

Like most other Gothic writers, Poe knows that terror and horror are social and relational rather than original or private.[42] All humans struggle against the same basic fears. Such battles prove necessary because they help us to confront life's unpleasant realities. Running from fear might even produce unhealthy consequences. Poe feels that "the attempt to escape may only intensify . . . horror."[43] One brief example from Poe's fiction illustrates this point. In "Usher," Roderick manages to bring about his own madness and death by refusing to face and conquer fear. The tale traces the history of his gradual descent into the realm of terror and madness. He becomes a passive victim of "the grim phantasm." Perhaps his situation would have been different if he had earlier faced his fears bravely. Instead he waited helplessly for fear and superstition to annihilate him.

Poe advises his readers not to retreat in the face of fear. Although enduring stress often proves painful, Poe, along with D.H. Lawrence, knows that "the human soul must suffer its own disintegration, consciously, if ever it is to survive."[44] Encountering boldly the demons lurking in the dungeons of the mind becomes the first step in exorcising these troublesome creatures. No doubt Poe desired to show his readers the necessity of navigating the tempests of life.[45] Fear can produce knowledge and courage if one exhibits a certain amount of tenacity.

The strategy of fear devised by Poe depends upon his knowledge of nineteenth-century readers and their popular tastes. Familiar with the operation of the mind, Poe relies on the horror-appeal present in human thought. Fear intrigues as it frightens us. Aware of the terror tale's popularity, Poe uses fear as the bait to attract readers into his Gothic world. To obtain the best possible results, Poe deliberately takes advantage of the particular fears present in the typical nineteenth-century mind. Knowledge of these "phobic pressure points" allows Poe to produce tales directed toward a reader's psychic weaknesses. He understands what specific fears exist in his contemporaries and accordingly exploits them. A discussion of Stephen King's *Danse Macabre* and Benjamin Rush's *Diseases of the Mind* may serve to elaborate the particular fears lodged within the minds of Poe's readers.

NOTES

1. Edgar Allan Poe, *Collected Works of Edgar Allan Poe*, ed. Thomas Ollive Mabbott (Cambridge, Mass.: The Belknap Press of Harvard University Press, 1978), Vol. 2, p. 403. All references to Poe's tales are taken from this edition.

2. Edgar Allan Poe, *The Complete Works of Edgar Allan Poe*, ed. James A. Harrison (New York: Thomas Y. Crowell, 1902; rpt. AMS Press, 1975), Vol. 17, pp. 263-264.

3. Harrison, p. 264.

4. P. Pendleton Cooke, "Edgar A. Poe," *The Recognition of Edgar Allan Poe: Selected Criticism Since 1829*, ed. Eric W. Carlson (Ann Arbor: University of Michigan Press, 1966), p. 26.

5. Edward Hungerford, "Poe and Phrenology," *American Literature* 2 (November 1930): 217.

6. Edmund Burke, *A Philosophical Enquiry into the Origin of Our Ideas of the Sublime and the Beautiful* (London: R. & J. Dodsley, 1757; rpt., New York: Columbia University Press, 1958), p. 57. See also Kent Ljungquist, *The Grand and the Fair: Poe's Aesthetics and Pictorial Techniques* (Potomac, Md.: Scripta Humanistica, 1984), pp. 48-50, 52-53, 195-203; and Craig Howes, "Burke, Poe, and 'Usher': The Sublime and Rising Woman," *ESQ: A Journal of the American Renaissance* 13 (1985): 173-189.

7. N. Bryllion Fagin, *The Histrionic Mr. Poe* (Baltimore: The Johns Hopkins Press, 1949), p. 31.

8. Paul Lewis, "Laughing at Fear: Two Versions of the Mock Gothic," *Studies in Short Fiction* 15 (Fall 1978): 413.

9. T.S. Eliot, "From Poe to Valery," in Carlson, p. 213.

10. G.R. Thompson, *Poe's Fiction: Romantic Irony in the Gothic Tales* (Madison: University of Wisconsin Press, 1973), p. 9.

11. For views assessing Poe as a creator of simultaneous serious and comic Gothicism, see Richard P. Benton, "Is Poe's 'The Assignation' a Hoax?," *Nineteenth-Century Fiction* 18 (September 1963): 193-197; and Benjamin Franklin Fisher

IV, "To 'The Assignation' from 'The Visionary' and Poe's Decade of Revising," *Library Chronicle* 39 (Spring 1973): 89-105; 40 (Winter 1976): 221-251; "Poe and the Art of the Well Wrought Tale," in his *Poe at Work: Seven Textual Studies* (Baltimore: The Edgar Allan Poe Society, 1978), pp. 5-12; "Blackwood Articles à la Poe: How to Make a False Start Pay," *Revue Des Langues Vivantes* 39 (Winter 1973): 418-432; and "Playful 'Germanism' in 'The Fall of the House of Usher,'" *Ruined Eden of the Present--Hawthorne, Poe, and Melville: Critical Essays in Honor of Darell Abel*, ed. G.R. Thompson and Virgil L. Locke (W. Lafayette, Ind.: Purdue University Press, 1981), pp. 355-374.

12. Taylor Stoehr, "'Unspeakable Horror' in Poe," *South Atlantic Quarterly* 78 (Summer 1979): 329.

13. Fred Lewis Pattee, *The Development of the American Short Story* (New York: Harper and Brothers, 1923; reprint ed., New York: Biblo and Tannen, 1966), p. 138. See also Walter Kendrick, *The Thrill of Fear: 250 Years of Scary Entertainment* (New York: Grove Weidenfeld, 1991), pp. 174-175.

14. See. Dudley R. Hutcherson, "Poe's Reputation in England and America, 1850-1909," *American Literature* 14 (November 1942): 216; David R. Saliba, *A Psychology of Fear: The Nightmare Formula of Edgar Allan Poe* (Lanham, Md.: University Press of America, 1980), p. 4; and J. Gerald Kennedy, *Poe, Death, and the Life of Writing* (New Haven: Yale University Press, 1987).

15. Arthur Voss, *The American Short Story: A Critical Survey* (Norman: University of Oklahoma Press, 1973), p. 53.

16. Norman Foerster, *American Criticism* (Boston: Houghton Mifflin, 1928), p. 27.

17. H.P. Lovecraft, *Supernatural Horror in Literature* (New York: B. Abramson, 1945; rpt., New York: Dover, 1973), p. 53.

18. Edith Birkhead, *The Tale of Terror* (New York: E.P. Dutton, 1920), p. 213.

19. Lowry Nelson, Jr., "Night Thoughts on the Gothic Novel," *Yale Review* 52 (December 1962): 238.
20. See David E.E. Sloane, "Usher's Nervous Fever: The Meaning of Medicine in Poe's 'The Fall of the House of Usher,'" *Poe and His Times: The Artist and His Milieu*, ed. Benjamin Franklin Fisher IV (Baltimore: The Edgar Allan Poe Society, 1990), pp. 146-153.
21. Montague Summers, *The Gothic Quest* (London: Fortune Press, 1938; rpt., New York: Russell and Russell, 1964), p. 37.
22. See Birkhead, p. 221; and Mary Maurita Redden, *The Gothic Fiction in the American Magazines (1765-1800)* (Washington, D.C.: Catholic University of America Press, 1939), p. 155.
23. Kay Mussell, "Gothic Novels," *Handbook of American Popular Culture*, ed. M. Thomas Inge (Westport, Conn.: Greenwood Press, 1978), p. 151.
24. Joanna Russ, "Somebody's Trying to Kill Me and I Think It's My Husband: The Modern Gothic," *Journal of Popular Culture* 6 (Spring 1973): 685.
25. G.R. Thompson, ed., *Romantic Gothic Tales: 1790-1840* (New York: Harper and Row, 1979), p. 9. See also Benjamin Franklin Fisher IV, *The Gothic's Gothic: Study Aids to the Tradition of the Tales of Terror* (New York and London: Garland Publishing, Inc., 1987), for indications of varied responses to Gothicism.
26. See Jerry A. Herndon, "Poe's 'Ligeia': Debts to Irving and Emerson," and Stanton Garner, "Emerson, Thoreau, and Poe's 'Double Dupin,'" *Poe and His Times*, ed. B.F. Fisher IV, pp. 113-129; 130-145; and Joan Dayan, *Fables of Mind: An Inquiry into Poe's Fiction* (New York: Oxford University Press, 1987), pp. 210-223.
27. Oral Sumner Coad, "The Gothic Element in American Literature Before 1835," *Journal of English and Germanic Philology* 24 (January 1925): 72.

28. James M. Keech, "The Survival of the Gothic Response," *Studies in the Novel* 6 (Summer 1974): 134.
29. Philip P. Hallie, *The Paradox of Cruelty* (Middletown, CT: Wesleyan University Press, 1969), p. 64.
30. Devendra P. Varma, *The Gothic Flame* (London: Arthur Barker Ltd., 1957), p. 130.
31. G.R. Thompson, ed., *The Gothic Imagination: Essays in Dark Romanticism* (Pullman: Washington State University Press, 1974), p. 3.
32. Barton Levi St. Armand, *The Roots of Horror in the Fiction of H.P. Lovecraft* (New York: Dragon Press, 1977), p. 3.
33. Robert Hume, "Gothic vs. Romantic: A Revaluation of the Gothic Novel," *PMLA* 84 (March 1969): 285.
34. Varma, pp. 209-210. See also Benjamin Franklin Fisher IV, "The Residual Gothic Impulse: 1824-1873," in *Horror Literature: A Core Collection and Reference Guide*, ed. Marshall B. Tymn (New York: R.R. Bowker, 1981), pp. 187-200.
35. Burton R. Pollin, "Poe 'Viewed and *Reviewed*': An Annotated Checklist of Contemporaneous Notices," *Poe Studies* 13 (December 1980): 17-28.
36. David Punter, *The Literature of Terror: A History of Gothic Fiction from 1765 to the Present Day* (New York: Longman, 1980), p. 202.
37. Sidney P. Moss, *Poe's Literary Battles* (Durham: Duke University Press, 1963), pp. 247-248.
38. Edgar Allan Poe, *Marginalia*, with an introduction by John Carl Miller (Charlottesville: University Press of Virginia, 1981), p. 193. See also Burton R. Pollin, ed. *Collected Writings of Edgar Allan Poe*: Volume 2, *The Brevities*, (New York: Gordian Press, 1985), p. 377.
39. Regarding Poe and popular taste see Hutcherson, p. 233; David K. Jackson, *Poe and the Southern Literary Messenger* (Richmond: Dietz Printing Co., 1934), p. 84; J. Lasley Dameron, *Popular Literature: Poe's Not-so-soon Forgotten Lore* (Baltimore: The Edgar Allan Poe Society, 1980);

Benjamin Franklin Fisher IV, "More Pieces in the Puzzle of Poe's 'The Assignation,'" *Myths and Reality: The Mysterious Mr. Poe*, ed. Benjamin Franklin Fisher IV (Baltimore: The Edgar Allan Poe Society, 1987), pp. 59-88; Barton Levi St. Armand, "The 'Mysteries' of Edgar Poe: The Quest for a Monomyth in Gothic Literature," in Thompson, *The Gothic Imagination*, p. 69; and Napier Wilt, "Poe's Attitude Toward His Tales: A New Document," *Modern Philology* 25 (August 1927): 105. Concerning Poe's understanding of the mind see James W. Gargano, "The Question of Poe's Narrators," in Carlson, p. 316; Pamela J. Shelden, "'True Originality': Poe's Manipulation of the Gothic Tradition," *American Transcendental Quarterly* 29 (Winter 1976): 75; Robert Shulman, "Poe and the Powers of Mind," *ELH* 37 (June 1970): 245; and Richard Wilbur, "The House of Poe," in Carlson, p. 260.

40. Consult Hallie, p. 79; Kent Ljungquist, "Burke's *Enquiry* and the Aesthetics of 'The Pit and the Pendulum,'" *Poe Studies* 11 (December 1978): 28; Jane Lundblad, *Nathaniel Hawthorne and the European Literary Tradition* (Upsala: Almquist & Wiksells, 1946; rpt., New York: Russell and Russell, 1965), p. 81; Rudolph Otto, *The Idea of the Holy*, trans. John Harvey (London: Oxford University Press, 1952), pp. 12-45; and Varma, p. 255.

41. Terry Heller, "Poe's 'Ligeia' and the Pleasures of Terror," *Gothic* 2 (Spring 1980): 46. See also Heller's *The Delights of Terror: An Aesthetics of the Tale of Terror* (Urbana: University of Illinois Press, 1987), pp. 193-195, 196-197.

42. Eve Kosofsky Sedgwick, "The Characters in the Veil: Imagery of the Surface in the Gothic Novel," *PMLA* 96 (March 1981): 256.

43. Jay L. Halio, "The Moral Mr. Poe," *Poe Newsletter* 1 (October 1968): 24.

44. D. H. Lawrence, "Edgar Allan Poe," in Carlson, p. 111.

45. Joseph M. Garrison, Jr., "The Function of Terror in the

Work of Edgar Allan Poe," *American Quarterly* 18 (Summer 1966): 146.

Chapter 2

Aesthetic and Scientific Theories: Stephen King, Benjamin Rush, and Fear

STEPHEN KING ON HORROR

Before examining nineteenth-century scientific thought regarding madness and fear, we should scrutinize the concept of horror envisioned by Stephen King in *Danse Macabre* (1981). This popular contemporary horror writer has formulated a theory which, applied to Poe's fiction in conjunction with the medical opinions of Benjamin Rush, allows us to understand and appreciate the well-developed fear formula used by Poe in his Gothic fiction. King's thoughts concerning the art of the macabre show how creators of terror tales attempt to ensnare their audiences. Although *Danse Macabre* deals specifically with horror tales and films appearing between 1950 and 1980, the ideas King presents shed light on works of terror produced long before that period. Similar if not identical notions of horror no doubt existed in the mind of Poe.

King analyzes horror film and fiction. Such forms of popular entertainment work on two levels. The first level rests on the artist's ability to lure his audience with flashy surface devices. An author or director might use bizarre physical cruelties or morally repulsive situations toward effecting the desired results.

As a fisherman relies on a tempting lure to attract large fish, so must the writer of macabre pieces coax his readers into entering the world of terror. Catching the eye of the victim, however, is only half the task. The writer must be certain to establish groundwork firmly to guarantee complete success. Here the second level in the strategy of horror art comes into play. Disregarding the belief that the work of horror depends solely on its fantastic, repulsive, or supernatural elements, King shows the true focus for the creator of such art:

> The work of horror really is a danse--a moving, rhythmic search. And what it's looking for is the place where . . . the viewer or reader live[s] at [his] most primitive level. . . . Is horror art? It achieves the level of art simply because it is looking for something beyond art, something that predates art: it is looking for what I would call phobic pressure points.[1]

Such pressure points exist as terminals of fear residing deep within the subconscious of every person. In order to reach as large an audience as possible a director or writer must first study the human mind and discover its weaknesses. Concentrating on these vulnerabilities, the artist provides himself or herself with a knowledge of the fears present in members of a particular society. As we have seen, the magnetic power of fear draws the reader toward it. The act of facing fear becomes pleasurable and delightful. Since audiences respond instinctively to fear the horror tale must use it to insure the reader's acceptance of the story and participation in it.

An awareness of the phobic pressure points possessed by readers of a particular time period proves vital to the artist working in the horror genre. Both individual and national fears exist in the mind. King feels that "the creator of a horror story is able to unite the conscious and subconscious with one potent idea" (p. 20). Once he has done so the writer manages to bring the deeply submerged phobic pressure point to the surface and forces his audience to struggle against it. The writer calls the reader's attention to his once secret fears and the reader faces the feelings aroused by his recognition of his own psychic soft spots. Horror succeeds only insofar as it touches the secret chords present in the audience. A writer should realize that "horror does not horrify unless the reader or viewer has been *personally touched* [my italics]. . . . Horror in real life is an emotion that one grapples with . . . all alone" (p. 25). Fear separates a reader from his fellows. He endures whatever terror lurks in the forest by himself. The writer knows this isolation and strives to learn what particular horrors will potentially isolate the reader. As King posits, "the business of creating horror is much the same as the business of paralyzing an opponent with the martial arts--it is the business of finding vulnerable points and then applying pressure there" (p. 77). Later we shall see how Poe relies on the vulnerable points in the nineteenth-century mind as he creates his tales of horror.

Earlier I discussed the positive results brought about by horror fiction. The tale of terror can serve man by assisting him in mastering his fear. King expresses a similar idea in *Danse Macabre*:

> The melodies of the horror tale are simple and repetitive, and they are the melodies of disestablishment and disintegration, but . . . the ritual outletting of these emotions seems to bring things back to a more stable and constructive state again. (p. 26)

Viewed in this light, the horror story becomes rewarding and magical. It permits the reader to observe death and monstrosity and to master innate fears of them. The fiction of horror proves valuable because it reaffirms the idea of order. According to King, the main purpose of the horror story is to stress the value of the norm (p. 368). Stories that illustrate the consequences of sojourns in the land of taboo permit one to recognize the importance of the standards which help protect and maintain civilized society. Far from acting as sermons on the perverse, all horror tales concern themselves with improving the state of society and the well-being of the mind.

Can a theory such as that proposed by King help us to appreciate better the fiction of Poe? As his tales and literary criticism demonstrate, Poe possesses a microscopic power of analysis.[2] Although he refuses to sermonize in his works, Poe suggests how true art can serve its society. Exploring the phobic pressure points of the readers supports the writer in attracting an audience. The members of the audience, in turn, can benefit from such fiction by reacting to the supernal beauty present in the true work of art. Reading a horror tale prompts one to acknowledge his own fears. Poe's awareness of power in fear prohibits him from suggesting that fear can be eliminated; scientists themselves fail to offer such an opinion. Poe does believe in the mind's ability to master its reservations. As the nineteenth-century psychologists Benjamin Rush and John Conolly state, one must face fear if he ever hopes to avoid being overpowered by it. Analysis of the mind leads Poe to a similar conclusion. By discussing the terrors of the soul Poe hopes to bring the mind, in the words of King, "to a more stable and constructive state." The value of such literature as is aimed toward this goal is immense.

Other ideas presented by King facilitate our understanding of Poe's fiction. Discussing all forms of horror art, King formulates two categories into which we can place such works:

> All tales of horror can be divided into two groups: those in which the horror results from an act of free and conscious will . . . and those in which the horror is predestinate, coming from outside like a stroke of lightning. (p. 71)

In Poe's tales much horror arises from internal sources. The presence of fear in the human mind creates horrors for Poe's protagonists because they for the most part are consciously unable to confront their fear. They expect the worst, and, for the most part, they receive what they expect. Innate forces dictate their responses to the situations in which they find themselves. Many of the characters in Poe's Gothic tales tremble at the thought of standing up to fear and become the victims of the terrors rooted in their brains. Fears arising from within present more serious problems than those originating from without because they boggle the mind and prevent its proper functioning. Such fears may even become exaggerated and lead to more unpleasant circumstances as the mind attempts to combat them.

Earlier we saw how some critics believe that Poe's fiction is unrealistic; they feel that many of the characters and events appearing in these tales suggest, at the very least, great improbability. King presents an opinion concerning horror fiction that vindicates Poe from such charges. Discussing the primary aim of the horror writer, King remarks that he uses such archetypes as the werewolf or vampire not as mythical figures but as representations of reality (p. 88). Although these creatures spring from legends centuries old, they depict actual and timeless mental proclivities. Writers rely on such devices to present their own views on psychic realities. When we look beyond the surface horror of the vampire mangling the neck of its victim and the God-fearing man becoming a wolf craving flesh when the full moon beckons, we discover the true roots of horror--which lie in the mind's darker confines. Events occurring in Poe's fiction are no different. The crack in Roderick Usher's house and the eyes of Ligeia terrify the reader because they strike at his fear like some poisonous serpent. Surface details become images of mental realities. Despite his use of myth, the horror writer confronts the reality of human behavior.

An awareness of phobic pressure points permits the writer to use his reader's fears to his own advantage. The presence of actual individual and societal fears in a tale or novel creates belief for a reader as he peruses the work. Fear, in other words, contributes to credibility in certain literature. No doubt aware

of a similar notion, Poe in his fiction uses those particular fears
that lie in the minds of his contemporaries. To discover the
nature of such fears, we must investigate some nineteenth-
century psychological opinions with which Poe was familiar.

BENJAMIN RUSH AND NINETEENTH-
CENTURY THEORIES

The American mind of the early nineteenth century sought
eagerly to gain new knowledge. Possessing strong inquisitiveness,
Americans became fascinated by the various scientific discover-
ies made during the period.[3] Edgar Poe was no exception; he
"was a reader of scientific works and was to show all his life a
keen interest in them."[4] Poe found particularly intriguing those
works discussing diseases of the human mind. Many of his
stories deal with different forms of mental aberrations, and the
effectiveness of these tales depends upon the medical theories
that provided Poe with a solid scientific basis for such creations.

Poe attempts to use science in his criticism, poetry, and
fiction. Walker comments on Poe's use of science and medicine
and concludes that such sources help to infuse his works with
the sense of reality:

> It is known that Poe was a keen student of current
> scientific opinion including medicine, and it is extremely
> unlikely that he could have written with such convincing
> realism and accuracy about madness and crime had he
> not been familiar with the opinions of "mental philoso-
> phers" then in vogue . . . like Benjamin Rush. . . . [5]

In addition to speculating on the relationship between scientific works and the reality they contribute to Poe's works dealing with mental derangement, Walker's remarks also reinforce Poe's familiarity with the theories of Benjamin Rush, an important medical figure in the early nineteenth century. Despite Poe's failure to mention Rush or his works in his writings, scholars believe that he knew Rush's works and theories.[6] At one time a resident of the City of Brotherly Love himself, Poe must have been aware of the famous Philadelphian whose theories helped create modern American psychology.

Benjamin Rush wrote on a variety of subjects. His books, including *Directions for Preserving the Health of Soldiers, Thoughts upon Female Education,* and *Consideration of the Injustice and Impolicy of Punishing Murder by Death,* reveal the wide range of his topics. As a medical man Rush often reflects the ideas of the eighteenth century. His reputation among his peers suffered greatly because he advocated such primitive cures as bloodletting and purges.[7] Remaining a controversial figure in the medical world, the one-time Physician General of the Continental Army became a good friend of John Adams. The Declaration of Independence bears Rush's signature. One of the founders of the American Republic, Rush directed his thought toward all areas of human endeavor.

Despite his medical methods and political thought, Rush's fame depends more on the popularity of his most famous book, *Medical Inquiries and Observations upon the Diseases of the Mind,* published in 1812. This monumental work broke ground for the new field of psychiatry. The "mental philosophers" of previous generations viewed insanity as a form of intentional evil. As his biographer indicates, "Rush recognized deviant behavior as illness rather than deliberate wickedness and thus helped lay the groundwork for the modern conception of personality disorder."[8] Although somewhat archaic when it came to the treatment of physical maladies, Rush in *Diseases of the Mind* presents a relatively modern theory concerning the nature of mental illness.

As we turn our attention toward *Diseases of the Mind*, we need to understand the theory of fear formulated by Rush. He discusses this emotion in a work concerned with mental "diseases." To Rush, then, fear is a form of madness. The person controlled by fear becomes to a greater or lesser degree mentally deranged. Infected thoughts cloud a patient's perceptions as the understanding deteriorates. Hoping that his work "may be the means of lessening a portion of some of the greatest evils of human life,"[9] Rush strives to understand better the relationship between the causes of and cures for madness.

Earlier we saw how horror tales may lead a reader to confront and perhaps even master his fears. Admitting his possession of certain fears that lead to irrational thoughts assists the reader in overcoming his anxieties. The horror writer uses fear as a type of inoculation. The carefully controlled, less potent germs of fear present in the terror tale permit the reader to increase his resistance to the stronger, uncontrolled manifestations of this emotion. Rush too acknowledges that at times fear proves beneficial:

> I know it has been said in favour of madness being an ideal disease, or being seated primarily in the mind, that sudden impressions from fear, terror, and even ridicule have sometimes cured it. This is true, but they produce their effects only by the *healthy* [my italics] actions they induce in the brain. (p. 17)

Rush presents a scientific basis for the theory of fear as anodyne. Such an opinion no doubt strengthened Poe's beliefs relative to the use of fear in his fiction.

In his second chapter Rush speculates on the two basic causes of intellectual derangement: those which act directly on the body and those which act indirectly on the body through the medium of the mind. Physical stimuli include tumors, abscesses, epilepsy, alcohol, or drugs. Some mental causes that affect the body are intense study or frequent and rapid transitions of the mind from one subject to another. These ideas of Rush's show how physical and mental agents together cause mental illness. Reinforcing this concept, he speculates that the understanding is affected by impressions acting primarily upon the heart (pp. 38-39). He lists fear and terror as two of the feelings that influence both body and mind. Like Edmund Burke, Rush believes that fear influences mental and physical processes. When respiration or heartbeat increases in the face of danger, the mind often cannot rationally view the stress-producing scene. Madness results from such mental lapses.

After discussing various causes of madness including heredity, climate, and a too-active imagination, Rush defines hypochondriasis. This condition features an error in opinion and conduct upon one subject only, with soundness of mind upon all or nearly all other subjects (p. 74). Frequently fear becomes the subject upon which the mind fails to act reasonably. Various symptoms accompany this state. The victim afflicted with hypochondriasis suffers acute distress. He often believes that he has a living animal in his body, or feels that he has inherited the soul of some fellow creature through the process of transmigration. Rush writes that "the lightest noises, such as the grating of a door upon its hinges, or its being opened and shut suddenly produce . . . anger or terror" (p. 83). Although he often appears cheerful, the victim eventually feels no comfort at the thought of life's prospects. Love, friendship, and affection do nothing to help such minds. As my next chapter will demonstrate, many of the characters in Poe's stories exhibit identical symptoms.

Commenting on the various stages of madness, Rush discusses the nature of what he terms "mania." The most serious of the three stages of general intellectual derangement, mania in its highest grade produces erroneous perception. A manic individual mistakes the persons and objects around him and perceives threats where none exist. Rush's theory anticipates an idea expressed by one of Poe's contemporaries, John Conolly, who theorizes that fear arises from the mind's inability to check the ramblings of the imagination. Conolly believes that the imagination "hurries men towards errors from which nothing but the greatest vigilance of their attention and comparison can preserve them."[10] The mind tends to exaggerate the power of fear, yet madness arising from superstitious fears is as real as any other type of insanity. In Conolly's opinion, mere aggravations of little weaknesses often produce insanity (pp. 166-167). Agreeing with Rush, he knows that fear exists as a form of mental illness:

> Regard a man who is wholly under the influence of fear. His mind is taken up with the strong impression made by the object feared. He has no attention for other objects; he cannot remember various means of defense or escape which he will think of when the danger has passed. He cannot compare one circumstance with another. He flies with precipitation, or he waits to be destroyed, or he does what hastens his destruction; he is, for the time, deprived of reason. How different is the situation of the man who has a sense of danger, but without fear. (pp. 226-227)

During this period fear maddens its victim. Once he manages to correct the erroneous judgment of his excited state, a man regains his sanity. Both Rush and Conolly emphasize the crucial role fear plays in determining the mind's condition. The specter of fear is real, and it often produces dreadful consequences. Resisting fear keeps the mind strong and active.

In the twelfth chapter of *Diseases of the Mind* Rush discusses derangement of the passions, recognizing two classes: those which impel us to good and those meant to defend us from real or supposed evil. Unfortunately passions are often subject to unreasonable, morbid excess. Love, grief, anger, and fear prove especially susceptible. When one of these emotions exerts an unusually strong dominance in the mind madness results.

Particularly important to my own study, Rush's ideas concerning fear provide Poe with vital scientific opinion. Commenting on what he considers the basic purpose of fear, Rush posits: "There are so much danger and evil in our world that the passion of fear was implanted in our minds for the wise and benevolent purpose of defending us from them" (pp. 324-325). As we have seen, however, fear often becomes uncontrollable and harmful. The objects of fear are essentially of two kinds: reasonable and unreasonable. Rush categorizes fear of death and fear of surgical operations as reasonable fears present in most minds. In the area of unreasonable fears he lists fear of thunder, darkness, ghosts, speaking in public, sailing, riding, and certain animals including cats, rats, or insects (p. 325). These fears discussed by Rush relate to the concept of the sublime formulated by Burke. Despite their unpleasant qualities, they also arouse the mind's curiosity. For example, the fear produced by thunder corresponds to the feelings of loudness and power that Burke believes help to create the sublime. Darkness relies on obscurity, privation, and difficulty. All of these fears, reasonable and unreasonable, trouble and amaze the mind. Rush advises doctors to help their patients confront rationally whatever fear threatens to overcome them. Discussion and study lead to the mastery of fear. Rush presents another opinion which may shed light on Poe's intentions:

> Great advantages may likewise be derived for the cure of fear by a proper application of the principle of association. A horse will seldom be moved by the firing of a gun or a drum beat if he hears them for the first time while he is eating. The same principle will work on the human mind to prevent or cure fear. (p. 333)

If readers associate fear with the usually pleasurable experience of perusing a work of literary art, they may increase their ability to conquer fear through the act of actually reading a tale. In such a case, fiction manages to squelch the demons of the mind and spurs readers to face the challenge of reality.

Diseases of the Mind provides Poe with a knowledge of the specific fears existing in the minds of his audience. Rush also allows Poe to realize how carefully measured doses of fear benefit the mind. Before studying just how Poe categorizes the various fears listed by Rush and breaks them down into related areas, we must first consult some of the twentieth-century concepts of fear to which the theories of Benjamin Rush gave birth.

MODERN PSYCHOLOGICAL PERSPECTIVES

Benjamin Rush exerted a strong influence on modern American psychologists who attempted to analyze the human reaction to fear. As a tribute to their predecessor, the members of the American Psychiatric Association use a portrait of Rush as their official seal. Although the treatment of fear and madness has improved significantly since the early nineteenth century, most psychologists agree with Rush's ideas concerning the types of fears present in the mind and the nature of this emotion.

Virtually all psychologists accept Rush's theory that most fears are strikingly unreasonable.[11] Rational discussion motivates a patient to face whatever fear plagues him and permits him to realize the absurd nature of his anxiety. Rachman believes that fear arises from irrational causes. He maintains that fears "can be acquired by exposure to a single intensely painful or frightening situation, but more probably acquired as a result of repeated exposures to *subtraumatic* [my italics] situations."[12] Such an opinion echoes Rush and also suggests the idea devised by Conolly regarding the sufferer's inability to make proper comparisons between various circumstances. Unable to recognize the ordinary nature of his predicament, the observer allows his mind to exaggerate the "danger" presented by various stimuli. Recurring situations of minor import, then, produce fear.

Modern psychologists acknowledge the existence and influence of many of the fears discussed by Rush. Marks, for example, comments on what Rush describes as the fear of speaking in public. Regarding this phobia, Marks remarks: "starting with innate mechanisms we learn that being looked at means being the object of another's attention and intention, so naturally the gaze of others triggers acute discomfort. . . ."[13] Like Rush, he also notes how certain conditions of light and space produce fear.[14] Marks concurs with Rush when he states that fear often proves beneficial because it allows one to react when threatened and avoid danger. Unfortunately the mind cannot always employ fear properly because it often perceives a threat where none exists. Using a term that did not appear in psychological treatises until the late nineteenth century, Marks describes such unreasonable fears as "phobias." He defines these manifestations of fear as "a special form of fear which is out of proportion to the demands of the situation [and] is beyond voluntary control."[15] Once the mind observes a certain stimulus and interprets it as something harmful it loses its ability to control the person's rational response to the particular circumstance. Madness often results in such a case.

Various statements made by modern psychologists provide us with interesting insights which we may apply to the fiction of Edgar Allan Poe. Rachman believes that fear results from an exposure to traumatic situations or the observation of people exhibiting fear.[16] If Poe manages to create realistic situations with which the reader can associate, the reader's fear will increase as he observes the responses of the characters in the tale. Aware of the magnetic quality of fear, Poe insures that his reader will feel the same fears which attack the story's protagonists and continue reading the work as he strives to explore and subdue his own mental weaknesses. Examining the means of reducing the effects of fear, Rachman mentions what he terms "flooding." This procedure involves exposing the patient to the fearful situation for a prolonged period of time (p. 73). Poe also "floods" his reader's mind with various fears in the hope of both attracting readers and helping them cope with fear. He understands that fear is both a response and a drive.[17] Concerned with his audience's reaction to fear, Poe also relies on man's instinctual need to experience this paradoxical emotion. Although fear terrifies, it can also strengthen. Well aware of fear's mode of operation, Gray states: "a frightened animal is most likely to try one of the three F's--freezing, flight, or fight. . . ."[18] Readers react similarly when they enter the world of fear fiction. Upon reading a tale and encountering incidents that touch the chords of their secret, personal fears, readers could conceivably have their minds frozen by such events. They would then proceed through the tale's world in a type of zombie trance that would prohibit them from analyzing their current predicament. They might instead close the book, which would be tantamount to fleeing the fear-ridden fictive land. Most readers, however, would opt for the third of Gray's reactions. Consciously resisting the demons of fear satisfies the reader immensely. With a firm knowledge of this fact in hand, Poe creates tales of horror and fear intended to appeal to his audience's feelings of curiosity and self-respect.

SPECIFIC FEARS IN POE'S GOTHIC FICTION

Poe's use of particular fears in his Gothic tales demonstrates his familiarity with the fears listed by Rush. Conceiving a plan of attack that relies on the reader's psychic vulnerabilities, he breaks down the fears isolated by Rush into various subdivisions. The fear of death (thanatophobia), for example, covers the subjects of mortality, the act of dying, the dead themselves, infinity, and the loss of individual identity after death.[19] Fear of surgery includes a wariness of illness and any sort of physical deformity. In Poe's tales the fear of thunder (brontophobia) also covers nature, foul weather, and any loud noise. Perhaps the most prominent of all the mind's fears is the fear of darkness (nyctophobia). Under this heading Poe includes the horror of enclosure (claustrophobia).[20] Most readers fear any type of ghost or any other form of supernatural visitor. The prospect of speaking in public places terrifies many individuals. Related to this dread are the fears of crowds and open spaces (agoraphobia), the evil eye, and strangers (xenophobia).[21] The reluctance of some people to go sailing or boating results from a fear of water (aquaphobia). Individuals who fear riding find themselves suspicious of horses (equinophobia) and heights (acrophobia). Fear arises in many people whenever they encounter certain animals (zoophobia) including cats (ailurophobia) and rats (murophobia). Another anxiety Poe employs, that dealing with insanity (dementophobia), is one of the most terrifying of human fears.[22] These phobias relate to the sources of the sublime described by Edmund Burke. The wonder produced by the feelings of obscurity, power, privation, vastness, infinity, difficulty, magnificence, and loudness attracts readers to stress-producing situations. In addition to using individual, personal fears, Poe takes advantage of national nineteenth-century phobic pressure points. Such national terrors include the fear of slave rebellions, wealth, and sex.[23] Poe incorporates numerous fears into his Gothic stories in order to frighten his audience from as many different angles as possible. As an artist conscious of contemporaneous medical opinions,[24] Poe employs the fears present in his reader's mind to produce a popular fiction rooted in aesthetic and scientific theory.

NOTES

1. Stephen King, *Danse Macabre* (New York: Everest House, 1981), p. 18.
2. Martin Farquhar Tupper, "American Romance," in Carlson, p. 19.
3. See Vernon Louis Parrington, *The Romantic Revolution in America, 1800-1860* (New York: Harcourt, Brace, 1927), p. iv; and David B. Davis, *Homicide in American Fiction, 1798-1860: A Study in Social Values* (Ithaca: Cornell University Press, 1957), p. 172.
4. Arthur Hobson Quinn, *Edgar Allan Poe: A Critical Biography* (New York: Appleton-Century-Crofts, 1941), p. 162.
5. I.M. Walker, "The 'Legitimate Sources' of Terror in 'The Fall of the House of Usher,'" *Modern Language Review* 61 (October 1966): 588. See also Robert D. Jacobs, *Poe: Journalist and Critic* (Baton Rouge: Louisiana State University Press, 1969), p. 296.
6. See, for example, David E.E. Sloane, "Early Nineteenth-Century Medicine in Poe's Short Stories" (M.A. thesis, Duke University, 1966); "Gothic Romanticism and Rational Empiricism in Poe's 'Berenice,'" *American Transcendental Quarterly* 19 (Summer 1973): 19-26; "Usher's Nervous Fever," *Poe and His Times*, ed. B.F. Fisher IV, pp. 146-153; David E. Whisnant, "Edgar Allan Poe's Study of Science" (M.A. thesis, Duke University, 1962); Carroll Laverty, "Science and Pseudo-Science in the Writings of Edgar Allan Poe" (Ph.D. dissertation, Duke University, 1951); Elizabeth Phillips, *Edgar Allan Poe: An American Imagination* (Port Washington, NY: Kennikat Press, 1979), p. 227.
7. Carl Binger, *Revolutionary Doctor: Benjamin Rush, 1746-1813* (New York: Norton, 1966), p. 227.
8. Binger, p. 280.
9. Benjamin Rush, *Medical Inquiries and Observations upon the Diseases of the Mind* (Philadelphia: Kimber and Richardson, 1812), p. 9.

10. John Connolly, *An Inquiry Concerning the Indications of Insanity* (London: John Taylor, 1830; rpt. London: Dawsons, 1964), p. 83.
11. Paul Errera, "Some Historical Aspects of the Concept of Phobia," *Psychiatric Quarterly* 36 (April 1962): 333.
12. Stanley Rachman, *Phobias: Their Nature and Control* (Springfield, Ill.: Charles C. Thomas, 1968), p. 39.
13. Isaac Marks, *Fears and Phobias* (New York: Academic Press, 1969), p. 30.
14. Marks, p. 32. For a complete list of fears see p. 104; and Stanley Rachman, *The Meanings of Fear* (Baltimore: Penguin, 1974), pp. 50-51.
15. Marks, p. 30.
16. Rachman, *The Meanings of Fear*, p. 14.
17. Calvin S. Hall and Gardner Lindzey, *Theories of Personality* (New York: John Wiley and Sons, 1970), p. 426.
18. Jeffrey A. Gray, *The Psychology of Fear and Stress* (London: Weidenfeld and Nicolson, 1977), p. 10.
19. Consult Joseph M. Defalco, "The Source of Terror in Poe's 'Shadow--A Parable,'" *Studies in Short Fiction* 6 (Fall 1969): 643-648, for a discussion of Poe's notion of death. See also Kennedy, *Poe, Death, and the Life of Writing*.
20. See Leonard W. Engel, "Identity and Enclosure in Edgar Allan Poe's 'William Wilson,'" *College Language Association Journal* 29 (September 1985): 91-99.
21. See Hallie, p. 67. The author feels that the eyes of the gothic villain represent destructive power.
22. Peter Obuchowski, "Unity of Effect in Poe's 'The Fall of the House of Usher,'" *Studies in Short Fiction* 12 (Fall 1975): 412.
23. Consult Jules Zanger, "Poe and the Theme of Forbidden Knowledge," *American Literature* 49 (January 1978): 536; and *Studies in the Literary Imagination* 7 (Spring 1974), iii-134. This special issue, "The Sources of Terror to the American Imagination," discusses at length those forces that nineteenth-century Americans believed might cause the

collapse of their young republic. We should also note that in *Diseases of the Mind* Rush treats the problems arising from unsuccessful love and seems to imply in a typically "proper" nineteenth-century fashion that physical love often causes mental distress.

24. David W. Butler, "Usher's Hypochondriasis: Mental Alienation and Romantic Idealism in Poe's Gothic Tales," *American Literature* 48 (March 1976): 5.

Chapter 3

Poe's Fiction of Fear

"METZENGERSTEIN," "MS. FOUND IN A BOTTLE," "THE ASSIGNATION," "SHADOW," AND "SILENCE"

Although some scholars view "Metzengerstein" as a mocking of the excesses of Gothic fiction,[1] the tale also represents Poe's serious attempt to depict some of the fears lodged within the human mind. Perhaps he "had in mind the wide audience attracted to Gothic fiction in contemporaneous magazines."[2] In addition to creating a story that would allow him to establish a good reputation among the reading public, he uses some of the fears listed by Rush as he strives to horrify his readers. In his first published Gothic tale Poe demonstrates mastery of the horror genre. He employs devices that would become his literary trademarks: the prophetic epigraph, the alert narrator, a consistent tone, chilling suspense, and a rousing climax. "Metzengerstein" must be considered the first step of Poe's journey into the domain of human fear.

In opening, the narrator remarks chillingly: "Horror and fatality have been stalking abroad in all ages" (18). Such words permit us to understand Poe's belief that the power of fear is timeless. Transcending the limits of temporal space, horror and fear endure. Such strong feelings are produced by the theory of metempsychosis, which is mentioned in the first paragraph. The idea of the transmigration of souls carries with it some horrible implications of which Poe is undoubtedly aware. Fear of the dead resides in all minds, as does fear of any type of supernatural visitor. Belief in metempsychosis permits the possibility of the dead returning to life. If a person performs a hateful act that results in the death of another, the murdered victim could conceivably return in corporeal form to avenge his murder. As I mentioned earlier, Rush remarks how the hypochondriacal patient often believes that he has inherited the soul of some fellow creature through the process of transmigration. Knowledge of this fact assists Poe to convey that in addition to stalking "abroad" in the mysterious regions of the interior of Hungary, fear lurks "within" in the curiously dark areas of the human mind. Whereas the reader recognizes immediately the importance of metempsychosis, young Frederick does not. The words of the ancient prophecy, in particular those dealing with "'the immortality of Berlifitzing'" (19), initially mean little to Baron Metzengerstein. Subsequent events lead the Baron (and us readers) to realize the strength of his enemy's supernatural power.

   In addition to the fear of the dead and the supernatural, Poe employs other specific human fears. We learn that "the inhabitants of the Castle Berlifitzing might look, from their lofty buttresses, into the very windows of the Palace Metzengerstein" (19). Old Wilhelm could glance into his rival's castle and observe Frederick's actions. The Baron would be susceptible to the Count's "evil eye" and sinister attention.[3] We can assume that Frederick is unnerved by this proximity and fears his neighbor's scrutiny. As the terrible fire rages through Berlifitzing's stables, Frederick becomes fascinated with a tapestry portraying a mysterious horse who once belonged to his rival's family.[4] At this point Poe incorporates the fear of horses into his tale. Combined with a fear of the evil eye, such anxiety intensifies the Baron's fear and he becomes spellbound by the tapestry. After viewing the fire that ravages his neighbor's stables, the Baron once again directs his attention toward the portrait of the enormous and unnaturally colored horse:

> To his extreme horror and astonishment, the head of the gigantic steed had . . . altered its position. The neck of the animal, before arched, as if in compassion . . . was now extended, at full length, in the direction of the Baron. The eyes, before invisible, now wore an energetic and human expression, while they gleamed with a fiery and unusual red. . . . (22-23)

Perishing in the fire, the Count assumes control of the horse in the tapestry and the "real" fiery-colored horse that appears after the Baron retreats in terror into the open air of the courtyard. Even after Berlifitzing dies, Metzengerstein remains susceptible to the evil eyes of the Count, eyes that penetrate the Baron's soul and see the guilt present there.

Frederick's terror increases as he notices the odd initials, "W.V.B.," branded on the forehead of this "extremely singular" animal. Guilt and fear bring about a change in his personality. He spends more time with the mysterious courser and realizes that the ferocious and demonic charger is more than a mere animal--it is his one-time enemy the Count. There occur "times when the young Metzengerstein turned pale and shrunk away from the rapid and searching expression of his earnest and human-looking eye" (28). Despite his fears, Frederick feels attracted to this supernatural steed: "Among all the retinue of the Baron . . . none were found to doubt the ardor of that extraordinary affection which existed on the part of the young nobleman for the fiery qualities of his horse" (28). This passage illustrates the relationship between fear and pleasure. Although fear creates discomfort, it also proves attractive. Metzengerstein encounters the feelings of power, magnificence, infinity, and difficulty when he confronts his horrible horse. Such qualities are sources of the sublime. The attraction-repulsion principle described by Burke comes into play clearly in this tale. The

Baron feels the effects of the paradoxical nature of fear and reacts to them in a typically human fashion. Poe has therefore created a fictive land that parallels that of the reader. The world of the characters becomes a world of living persons.[5]

Toward the conclusion the narrator states "how . . . intense is the excitement wrought in the feelings of a crowd by the contemplation of human agony . . ." (29). These words illustrate Poe's belief in the hypnotic and alluring nature of fear. As the Baron rides his hellish mount he struggles to master his anxieties. Instead he falls prey to agony and terror. Relying on the fear of horses and riding mentioned by Rush, Poe has this horse bear Frederick away amid the clamor of the tempest and the glare of the fire.

In the final paragraph Poe incorporates the fear of enclosure. Earlier he described Metzengerstein's apartment as one in which the Baron sat "buried" in thought, surrounded by gloomy tapestries. The horse's stall is called an "enclosure," and this image, coupled with the previous one, suggests the confines of the grave. In the conclusion, "A white flame still enveloped the building like a shroud . . ." (29). Such images show how the Baron becomes "buried" by his own hate and fear and by Berlifitzing's revenge. The dread of enclosure, the dead, the supernatural, the evil eye, and horses and riding used in the story show how at the beginning of his writing career Poe lays a firm foundation for the stories of fear that are still to come. Despite its similarities to "German" terror tales "Metzengerstein" relies on Poe's familiarity with nineteenth-century psychology and the terrors present in his audience's souls.

Unlike "Metzengerstein," which embodies many of the standard trappings of Gothic fiction, "MS. Found in a Bottle" features the sea as its setting, and is based on the idea of ocean adventure. Stories of the high seas were enormously popular during Poe's lifetime. "MS. Found," then, represents Poe's effort to use a much sought type of fiction that intrigues readers. Throughout this tale Poe also reveals his understanding of the mechanics of fear and of the beauty present in even the most terrifying situations.

As the story opens, the narrator goes to great pains to emphasize his lack of imagination. Revealing himself in such a manner he hopes to help his reader (who, we must recall, has allegedly found the bottle containing the story on some distant beach) believe the events chronicled in the manuscript. He writes: "Upon the whole, no person could be less liable than myself to be led away from the severe precincts of truth by the *ignes fatui* of superstition" (135). His is a logical mind that refuses to acknowledge the influence of emotion. The careful reader will note that the speaker is separated from his country and family. Referring to himself as a skeptic, he leads us to believe that he is isolated from two basic human emotions-- patriotism and love. In a sense, he appears to have enclosed himself in a tomb-like "pyrrhonism." He becomes "dead" to essential human feelings. As he has been "walled up" by his reliance on physical philosophy so too will he be entombed by the ship that eventually carries him to his death and an aware- ness of the emotional wonders of the universe. In this tale Poe cleverly suggests mental and physical enclosure.

The primary fears elicited by Poe's tale involve foul weather, nature, sailing, water, and darkness. The speaker writes of oddly shaped clouds, the sinister appearance of the moon, and the peculiar nature of the water. His "full presentiment of evil" (136) proves warranted when a terrific storm strikes the ship. A curious event occurs, however. For the time being, the force of the great wave has steadied the ship, which because of poor stowage had previously been in danger of capsizing. Despite the narrator's persistent fears, "the blast proved, in a great measure, the salvation of the ship" (137). A fearful act has produced beneficial results. Perhaps Poe suggests here that terrible situations might often assist an individual, provided he can place such events in proper perspective. The narrator seems at last capable of some display of emotion when he notices the terrific,

magnificent power of the mountainous waves. He glimpses the
inherent beauty present in the thundering sea that will soon
engulf him. He has looked briefly at the eternity into which a
watery tomb will soon place him.

Fear of darkness and its accompanying obscurity terrifies the
speaker and his sole companion, the Swede. A sun producing no
light insures that the survivors "were enshrouded in pitchy
darkness" and that "Eternal night continued to envelop us . . ."
(138-139). The diction suggests enclosure or interment. Darkness pervades and batters the speaker's mind with fear: "All
around were horror, and thick gloom, and a black sweltering
desert of ebony. Superstitious terror crept by degrees into the
spirit of the old Swede, and my own soul was wrapped up in
silent wonder" (139). Although he believes in the hopelessness
of his situation, the narrator continues to grow aware of the
intense spiritual beauty within his predicament.

As the ship hovers high atop waves one moment and then
flounders amid the depths of the whirlpool the next, our speaker
finds himself overcome by the dread of excessive heights and
depths. If we view this wildly lurching ship as an animal similar
to that appearing in "Metzengerstein," we observe again the fear
of riding. Like young Frederick, the sailor in "MS. Found" rides
toward his doom and a realization of his own past. After being
hurled onto the deck of the mysterious ship that crushes his own
vessel the speaker manages to hide in a dark hold from the
ghostly crew.[6] Secure in his "grave," he realizes that he has
been changed by his harrowing adventure: "A new sense--a new
entity is added to my soul" (141). Whereas the crew appears
unable to see, the narrator's vision increases to the point where
he perceives his growing awareness of eternity. The word
"discovery" that he paints on the folded studding sail describes
adequately the unusual purpose of his voyage.

Terror continues to plague the sailor. When he comments
"we are surely doomed to hover continually upon the brink of
eternity, without taking a final plunge into the abyss" (143), he
appears to lament his inability to enter the placid realm of the

beyond. His recognition of strange metaphysical forces increases. He is reluctant to dismiss the purely physical causes for the ship's dangerous plight. Fear has infected his mind, but he still sees the curious beauty present in all the events that threaten his existence:

> To conceive the horror of my sensations is, I presume, utterly impossible; yet a curiosity to penetrate the mysteries of these awful regions, predominates even over my despair, and will reconcile me to the most hideous aspect of death. It is evident that we are hurrying onwards to some exciting knowledge--some never-to-be-imparted secret, whose attainment is destruction. (145)

The narrator, who has grown more emotional as the story develops, notices how the crew seems oblivious to the horrors around them. As the ship tosses on the waves and the roaring ocean prepares to engulf the ghostly vessel, the faces of the crewmen bear not the look of despair but of hope. Clearly, the knowledge and secret toward which the speaker sails deal with the existence of eternity. Previously schooled solely in the events of the physical world, the sailor, through fear, has been shown the spiritual reality that lies at the center of the universe. He is redeemed by terror. Death carries with it a knowledge of the ultimate source of the sublime. Transferring Gothic fiction from the sinister castle to the vast sea, Poe in "MS. Found" creates a fictive land that, like the world of his readers, relies on the mystifying powers of fear.[7]

Centering on one of the national phobic pressure points present in nineteenth-century readers, "The Assignation," unlike "Metzengerstein" or "MS. Found," centers on the emotionally unhealthy results of illicit love affairs. Despite the social unacceptability of such liaisons, readers in Poe's time (and our own) found such tales appealing. Poe uses other fears in this story. Besides the solicitude produced by extramarital soirees, he incorporates fears of death, darkness, and enclosure to create an atmosphere of Gothic doom.

The opening paragraphs establish the sense of tomb-like melancholy that eventually subdues the ill-fated stranger. Venice becomes "a star-beloved Elysium of the sea . . . whose . . . palaces look down with a deep and bitter meaning upon the secrets of her silent waters" (151). By comparing the Italian city to the Elysian plain, Poe evokes the notion of fetid death. The canals of Venice resemble the foul Charonian canal in mythology. Cold and shadow permeate the scene. The narrator describes the night as gloomy, lonely, and silent. Lights are not extinguished: they "die" away. Images of the tomb and death set the stage for the twin deaths that take place in the conclusion.

Like the terrified sailor in "MS. Found" this speaker finds himself drifting along a body of water when his gondolier, reacting to a woman's screams, drops his oar. The gondola wanders along the canal "like some huge and sable-feathered condor" (152), thereby resembling a large bird of death. When the child falls into the murky, foul-smelling waterway, the water closes over its victim and apparently buries the youngster. Poe informs us that the canal is silent. Such quiet resembles that of the grave. The Marchesa Aphrodite gasps in terror, but her husband, Mentoni, remains unmoved by the horrible scene unfolding before him. Described as old, intriguing, and Satyr-like, he becomes a type of demon who seems strangely comforted by the child's misfortune. Finding no pity or concern in her husband, the Marchesa in a puzzling action glances toward the old prison:

> but how could that lady gaze so fixedly upon it, when beneath her lay stifling her own child? Yon dark, gloomy niche, too, yawns right opposite her chamber window-- what, then, *could* there be in its shadows--in its architec- ture--in its ivy-wreathed and solemn cornices--that the Marchesa di Mentoni had not wondered at a thousand times before? (153)

From this vault-like niche the stranger dives into the water and saves the child. The imagery used to describe the building from which the stranger emerges suggests a mausoleum. His beneficent action, however, is eclipsed by the ominous atmosphere of death that fills the scene with lamentable gloom. Stepping out from a "tomb" that serves to imprison man's corporeal essence, the stranger will soon return to the realm of the shadows when he commits suicide. He leaves a tomb early in the story and prepares to enter a grave at the conclusion. The Marchesa also suggests the presence of death. As she waits for a strong swimmer to rescue her baby, "a snowy-white and gauze-like drapery seemed to be nearly the sole covering to her delicate form . . ." (152). Such "clothing" resembles a burial shroud. Stiff and pale, she assumes the death-like appearance of a marble statue. Later she will again grow rigid as a result of death's eternal grasp. Throughout the tale Poe gives us the impression that the world of Venice becomes a colony for the domain of death. The narrator in this story, moreover, suggests the figure of death approaching as he glides in his gondola through the eerie canals toward the fated pair.

When her child is handed to her the Marchesa seems to return to life. Her cheeks grow red and she quivers as she beholds the infant's savior. Here we learn that Aphrodite's reaction may result from an illicit love connection with the handsome stranger:

> Why *should* that lady blush! To this demand there is no answer--except that, having left, in the eager haste and terror of a mother's heart, the privacy of her own *boudoir*, she has neglected to enthrall her tiny feet in their slippers, and utterly forgotten to throw over her Venetian shoulders that drapery which is their due. What other possible reason could there have been for her so blushing?--for the glance of those wild appealing eyes? for the unusual tumult of that throbbing bosom?-- for the convulsive pressure of that trembling hand?--that

hand which fell, as Mentoni turned into the palace,
accidently, upon the hand of the stranger. (155)

No doubt Poe's readers are not nearly as naive as his narrator.
In all likelihood the Marchesa's hand does not "accidently" touch
that of the stranger. We now realize why she earlier glanced
toward the prison niche: she awaited her lover. Later we shall
see how their affair culminates in mutual deaths.

Death imagery again plays a vital role when the narrator
visits the stranger's palazzo. Approaching the apartment he
notices its "gloomy, yet fantastic pomp" (156-157). Fear and
wonder fill his mind as he explores visually the odd decor of the
domicile. The stranger's wealth is obvious. Despite the valuable
treasures that fill the room, the speaker believes that much of
the splendor evident in the apartment mingles with a sense of
weirdness:

> Rich draperies in every part of the room trembled to the
> vibration of low, melancholy music, whose origin was not
> to be discovered. The senses were oppressed by mingled
> and conflicting perfumes, reeking up from strange
> convolute censers, together with multitudinous flaring
> and flickering tongues of emerald and violet fire. (157)

Wealth provides no genuine comforts for the stranger. The
draperies serve to enclose the viewer in a crypt, and the fires
suggest the memorial lamps present in tombs. We should note
that in Poe's fiction the room and its furnishings play an active
role in the story.[8] Here we see how a feeling of impending
death taints the otherwise beautiful chamber. As beams of
natural and artificial light combine to create a mysterious, almost
uncomfortable atmosphere, so does the stranger's inability to
separate natural and artificial love create discomfort for himself.
He experiences the sublime emotions of privation and difficulty
and longs for a love that in reality brings him intense pain. His
visitor notices "a certain air of trepidation--a degree of nervous

unction in action and in speech--an unquiet excitability of manner which appeared to me at all times unaccountable, and upon some occasions even filled me with alarm" (161). Discovering a somewhat "impure" poem written by his friend in which a man is separated from the woman he loves when she marries an old nobleman, the narrator receives a hint concerning his friend's plight. As the host reveals a painting hidden behind draperies his companion observes that it depicts the stunning figure of the Marchesa. In addition to emphasizing the ethereal beauty present in the picture, he notices that "there still lurked (incomprehensible anomaly!) that fitful stain of melancholy which will ever be found inseparable from the perfection of the beautiful" (164). Only after he learns that the Marchesa and her lover have committed suicide by poison can the narrator piece together at last the once perplexing mystery of the stranger's curious behavior. Unable to experience an open love in life, the stranger and the Marchesa hope to meet in the "hollow vale" of death.

Poe fills his tale of sinister love with images of death to show how such affairs, although sensually somewhat enjoyable, produce pain and sorrow. As the tale concludes we receive no indications that the lovers will meet once they have entered eternity. If we recall the tomb imagery that permeates the story, we must conclude that the two deaths carry with them the improbability of such a union taking place.[9] Other works by Poe, however, seem to present a more hopeful view of death.

The power of death also provides Poe with the central idea of "Shadow--A Parable". This terrifying tale, written in a beautiful, biblical prose, must have horrified Poe's readers. The tale initially paints a rather bleak picture of death and its domain that serves to provide a sound foundation for the human fear of death. Death appears as a gloomy shadow that dwells in the foul realm of Charon, the figure who ferries the dead into Hades. Despite this rather sullen description of the afterlife, Poe shows how the fear of death can and must be mastered. Using a prose reminiscent of the Bible, the ultimate book of hope, he

believes that human beings should view death as a passageway
leading to eternal life and companionship.

Little hope is evident as the tale opens, however. The words
of Oinos create an impression that haunts the entire piece: "Ye
who read are still among the living; but I who write shall have
long since gone my way into the region of shadows" (188). His
words describe an eternity that fails to coincide with that
presented by traditional Judeo-Christian commentators. He
believes that the streets in this mysterious land are not paved
with gold. Darkness instead rules this sinister kingdom. Here,
early in the tale, Poe plays on man's traditional fear of death
and his reluctance to enter any dark or enclosed space.

Oinos's recounting of the horrible pestilence that spread
across his homeland serves to introduce the fear of illness and
disease. Many of Poe's readers undoubtedly recalled their own
encounters with various epidemics that at one time or another
early in the nineteenth century befell the United States. They
feared that they might one day fall victims to the specter of
disease. They could sympathize with Oinos when he describes
his own reaction to the horrible plague that besieges the city of
Ptolemais: "The year had been a year of terror, and of feelings
more intense than terror for which there is no name upon the
earth" (189). Cosmic doom seems at hand and both the entire
planet and the creatures that inhabit it are overcome by a dark
feeling of dread. Even the heavens wear an ill aspect.

Fearful of death, Oinos and six associates enclose themselves
within a tomb-like hall, hoping to be spared.[10] Instead of acting
as a sanctuary, their shelter resembles a crypt: "Black draperies,
likewise, in the gloomy room, shut out from our view the moon,
the lurid stars, and the peopleless streets--but the boding and
memory of Evil, they could not be so excluded" (189). The room
fails to sequester Oinos and his fellows from death. Ironically,
this chamber seems to beckon the Great Shadow. Despite their
drunken revelry the seven men feel a certain "heaviness in the
atmosphere--a sense of suffocation. . . . A dead weight hung
upon us . . . and all things were depressed, and borne down

thereby . . ." (189). The black table at which they sit reflects the sullen images of the people in the chamber. Their songs become tunes of madness and their wine assumes the appearance of blood. The tomb imagery suggested earlier through Poe's appropriate diction becomes clearer when we learn that amid the seven comrades lies the rotting body of their acquaintance Zoilus.[11] A victim of the plague, this fetid corpse, horribly distorted by disease, seems to view scornfully the actions of Oinos and his friends. Zoilus appears "to take such interest in our merriment as the dead may haply take in the merriment of those who are to die. But although I, Oinos, felt that the eyes of the departed were upon me, still I forced myself not to perceive the bitterness of their expression . . ." (190). Why should the dead Zoilus view bitterly the actions of the entombed merrymakers? Having entered the domain of shadow himself he has realized the folly of attempting to avoid death. Wine and song can never ward off the death that awaits all mankind. Perhaps Zoilus also understands that the act of dying is not as ominous as it appears. Shaken by the message imparted by the enlightened eyes of the dead Zoilus, Oinos fails to grasp the meaning behind the corpse's expression. He continues to sing, hoping to avoid the fate toward which all living beings move.

Like the characters in "The Masque of the Red Death," Oinos and company fail to escape the grasp of death.[12] Impervious to the huge brass door, a strange figure enters the room as the songs of the occupants cease:

> from among those sable draperies where the sounds of the song departed, there came forth a dark and undefined shadow--a shadow such as the moon, when low in heaven, might fashion from the figure of a man: but it was the shadow neither of man, nor of God, nor of any familiar thing. (190)

Oinos fears to glance at the horrible specter because he realizes that it has come to claim the souls of seven more victims. Finally mustering enough courage, he questions the visitant and learns that it has indeed come from the land of death. What terrifies Oinos and his compatriots about the shadow's response is that it emerges not as from a single voice but as from thousands that they immediately recognize as belonging to many of their departed friends. No person can resist the death embrace. Oinos learns that death must be the universal fate of all living creatures. This realization horrifies while it illuminates.

The concluding words of "Shadow" show how the story becomes a work of hope. All individuals fear death. Destruction brought about by terrible pestilence proves especially horrible. Many people view this phenomenon as something dark and sinister. Yet as Poe's final sentence clearly states, the voices heard are those of friends. The act of dying remains frightening, but the world the dead must enter does not contain demons or devils but well-remembered and familiar companions. Dying leads one into a new state of existence. In this tale Poe demonstrates how the feelings of obscurity and infinity create tension in the minds of humans. In the true spirit of the religious parable, he also shows how fears and reservations can be conquered.

A companion piece to "Shadow," "Silence--A Fable" also examines the human reaction to death. This tale puzzles as many scholars today as it did during Poe's time. Exploring the underside of human consciousness, Poe seems to conceal and reveal simultaneously.[13] Should this story be read as satire, or does it present its subject seriously? A close reading allows one to recognize our author's serious implications, whatever comic propensities he mingled with them. In order to understand better the drift of this tale, we need to compare it with "Shadow." Each story depends on the other in the manner Milton's *L'Allegro* relies on *Il Penseroso*. In each, Poe presents an alternative view of death. As I mentioned above in regard to "Shadow," the strong apprehensions felt by humans as they contemplate the Grim Reaper can be mastered once they learn that death leads to eternal life. "Silence," however, offers no such reassurances. Poe's imagery and diction create a scene in which the quiet of the tomb conquers all. No familiar voices present themselves to comfort man.

The demon who relates the frightening chronicle to the speaker proves difficult to interpret. Relying on the human fear of the supernatural, Poe might intend the demon to be an actual creature from the realm of hell. As an emissary of Satan, he places his hand upon the speaker's head, just as a bishop anoints a new priest or confirms a new Christian. Such an action may also be the devil's way of initiating another member into the cult of death. Perhaps the demon represents the narrator's "irrational destructive side, a part of the self that exists close to the animal potential within all of us . . . and just as close to death."[14] Combining these two theories brings us closer to an understanding of the demon's function. This mysterious figure is as real as the fear of death. He shows man the fate that awaits him in the hope of terrorizing him. Although he is not subdued completely by the demon's presentation, the man believes that no solace or hope exists beyond the tomb. His own irrational fears seem to have the upper hand.

The first picture painted by the demon portrays the tumultuous qualities of nature. Dreary and convulsive, the rivers and water lilies seem to sigh as they contemplate their gloomy existence. We learn: "'the waters of the river have a saffron . . . hue'" (195), and this coloration connotes the idea of mourning and death. Trees rock restlessly in the forest although there is no wind. Poisonous flowers abound, and sinister gray clouds move west toward the land of the sunset and death. Rain turns into blood. A man enters and contemplates the desolation in the scene. The demon observes that although the man trembles he does not flee in terror. Perhaps he feels immune to the perils presented by such an episode because the chaotic noises he hears resemble closely the state of reality (life itself often becomes tempestuous and hectic). No storm conjured by the demon can completely terrify the man. He may weaken slightly, but, for the most part, he remains unmoved by natural occurrences. Poe suggests that desolation and commotion are natural conditions for man. We see in this tale how physical and psychic elements combine to establish a mutual relationship between space and observer.[15] In later tales, Poe will show how the powers of nature terrify and at times mock the actions of men. Here, however, much to the demon's dismay, the man masters his fear of harsh weather and loud noises.

Watching the scene from his tomb-like cover, the demon decides to employ a different extreme. Instead of attempting to horrify the man with chaos he will command that his minions become still. As desolation yields to soundlessness the man reacts as his tormentor hoped he would:

> "And mine eyes fell upon the countenance of the man, and his countenance was wan with terror. And, hurriedly, he raised his head from his hand, and stood forth upon the rock and listened. But there was no voice throughout the vast illimitable desert, and the characters upon the rock were SILENCE. And the man shuddered, and turned his face away, and fled afar off, in haste, so that I beheld him no more." (198)

What terrifies the man is the unnatural quiet that brings with it the darkness of the grave. Unable to accept a silence that appears infinite, the man must flee as he contemplates his own mortality. His trembling turns into shuddering as his fears gain control of his mind. Terrifying noises have become horrifyingly silent. The irrational demons of his mind emerge victorious.

The closing paragraph allows us to place the numerous images of death appearing in "Silence--A Fable" into perspective. Our narrator informs us that the "fable" related by the demon was told "as he sat by my side in the shadow of the tomb . . ." (198). Immensely satisfied with his unnerving tale, the devil laughs convulsively. His levity arises from his own realization of the hopelessness in the grave that awaits all humans. Incapable of sharing in the devil's delight, the narrator must ponder his own fate. Like his fellow human in the devil's story, he must separate himself from the demon and his associate the lynx and the terror and treachery they represent. Fear prevents him from entering the tomb and experiencing its excruciating silence. He fails to master the terrors lodged in his soul. Unlike "Shadow," "Silence" offers no hope for the human being seeking spiritual reassurance.

"BERENICE," "MORELLA," "LIGEIA," "THE FALL OF THE HOUSE OF USHER," AND "WILLIAM WILSON"

"Berenice" may be one of Poe's most puzzling explorations of the land of horror. On one level the story appears to rely on traditional vampire lore. Possibly, as he did in many other works, Poe intended his tale to satirize Gothicism.[16] Without altogether dismissing this opinion, we might with equal plausibility conclude that "Berenice" represents Poe's conscious effort to overwhelm his reader's mind with repulsive horror. This tale captures an audience through its use of various fears. In *Diseases of the Mind* Rush states that intense study often causes insanity. As we shall see, Egaeus' mind has been affected adversely by the mysterious book he reads. Like Hawthorne's Fanshawe and Rappaccini, he entombs himself in his studies and suffers accordingly. Viewing himself as a seer, he experiences "visions" of earth's misery; these eventually lead him toward one of the most infamous actions in Poe's tales. The extraction of Berenice's teeth disgusts many readers. Such an episode proves disturbing enough as we observe Egaeus' mutilation of a seemingly dead body. Learning subsequently that Berenice was alive when her mate performed his bizarre dentistry, the audience recoils in terror. Poe's use of the fears of premature burial (enclosure) and surgery strengthen the reader's misgivings. Like Faulkner's *Sanctuary*, "Berenice" in one respect becomes a potboiler.[17] Poe draws his readers into a domain of unspeakable horror. He realizes fully that by so doing he can increase the size of his audience and achieve for his tales and himself an unbounded popularity.

As the tale opens we perceive that Egaeus possesses a most subjective view of life. Drowned in despair, he feels that misery engulfs the entire planet. Revealing certain biographical facts, he comments that "there are no towers in the land more time-honored than my gloomy, gray, hereditary halls. Our line has been called a race of visionaries . . ." (209). The description suggests the "high" estate of Egaeus' family. Despite his apparent wealth, we hear that his domicile is gloomy and gray. This revelation, coupled with our knowledge about his family's beliefs, leads us to suspect that he will sooner or later engage in some nefarious activity. The sinister books comprising his library (which adumbrate those of Roderick Usher in *his* isolation) fill his mind with wild thoughts. This room becomes tomb-like in the sense that its book-covered walls insulate him from healthy contact with the outside world:

> it *is* wonderful what stagnation there fell upon the springs of my life--wonderful how total an inversion took place in the character of my commonest thought. The realities of the world affected me as visions . . . while the wild ideas of the land of dreams became, in turn,-- not the material of my every-day existence, but in very deed that existence utterly and solely in itself. (210)

Intense study has clouded Egaeus' mind. His perceptions are those of a mentally troubled individual, and his relationship with Berenice reflects his mental condition.

Unlike her cousin Egaeus, Berenice ventured frequently into the physical world. Hers was a life of carefree pleasure until she became a victim of disease. Both cousins, therefore, find themselves overcome by illness. Egaeus suffers from a mental sickness and Berenice endures the physical horrors produced by a form of epilepsy. Commenting on his own affliction, Egaeus provides the reader with valuable information that will help explain his subsequent actions. A curious "intensity of interest" befalls him whenever he contemplates ordinary objects:

> In my case, the primary object was *invariably frivolous*, although assuming, through the medium of my distempered vision, a refracted and unreal importance. . . . The meditations were *never* pleasurable; and, at the termination of the revery, the first cause, so far from being out of sight, had attained that supernaturally exaggerated interest which was the prevailing feature of the disease. (212)

This malady will manifest itself horribly when Egaeus later observes his cousin's teeth.

As she sinks deeper into the abyss of disease, the physical changes that occur in Berenice are carefully observed by the watchful eye of the diseased Egaeus. He discovers that her sickness has made him love her. This curious realization no doubt springs from his belief in the pervading nature of misery. Contemplating Berenice's suffering, Egaeus feels that she reflects the true nature of existence. Since he longs for distress, he can now bring himself to love his cousin who, to his troubled mind at least, becomes the personification of desolation and sorrow. Previously she seemed to linger in a land of dreams. Her life appeared illusory. Now she has assumed the air of reality. Although it troubles Egaeus somewhat, Berenice's pitiable condition draws him toward her. Her physical misery corresponds with that evident in the spiritual essence of the universe.

Up to this point in the tale Poe has not presented any truly repulsive details. He paves the way to a macabre conclusion by means of Berenice's mysterious entering of her cousin's library.

We now learn of Egaeus' most unusual interest in her teeth, which have suddenly assumed some sort of startling significance. Berenice's unexpected appearance (she seems to have materialized suddenly) startles Egaeus. Earlier in the tale Egaeus suggested that it was in this room that his mother died while giving birth to him. The volumes contained in this crypt-like library "bury" Egaeus' perception and reason. As his mother perished in this chamber so too has his ability to perceive reality. To his troubled mind Berenice appears rather ghastly, almost supernatural. Her teeth terrify him and he finds it impossible to forget them:

> I saw them *now* even more unequivocally than I beheld them *then*. The teeth!--the teeth!--they were here, and there, and every where, and visibly and palpably before me; long, narrow, and excessively white, with the pale lips writhing about them. . . . (215)

Many readers no doubt associate such a scene with traditional vampire stories. Perhaps Berenice *has* become a blood-crazed being, but we must recall Egaeus' mental condition. As a result of his sickness, he finds himself concentrating unnaturally on Berenice's teeth. In his crazed excitement he views the emaciated body of Berenice as some type of apparition. He later decides that only possession of her teeth will allow him to regain some semblance of reason.

After Berenice's death, Egaeus becomes disturbed by what he thinks is a dream. His memory concentrates excessively on the sounds of a shrieking female voice. Poe now incorporates the fears of premature burial and surgery into his story. In an attempt to relieve his anxiety, Egaeus has removed the teeth from what he thought was Berenice's corpse. Much to his dismay he discovered that she was not dead but merely suffering from a cataleptic fit. He had torn the teeth from his *living* cousin, a woman he had buried alive. Egaeus' action reveals, ironically, his attempt to regain sanity by violating the sanctity of the grave and the dignity of a corpse. Sloane believes that this episode results from Poe's familiarity with a theory of Benjamin Rush.[18] Rush suggests that certain diseases could be cured through the extraction of teeth. Aware of this belief, Poe has Egaeus attempt to cure not the physical illness of Berenice but his own mental derangement. Unfortunately for Egaeus, his studies have prevented his ability to think clearly, and his truly horrible action brings him no solace. Although the central character in this tale finds no relief, the author seems satisfied with his artistic creation. In a letter to Thomas White Poe explains that "Berenice" "originated in a bet that I could produce nothing more effective on a subject so singular, provided I treat it seriously."[19] Relying on the dread produced by so "singular" a subject, Poe insures that readers will read eagerly his tale of horror as they willfully explore the caverns of the mind.

Like "Berenice," "Morella" features a beautiful young lady who plays a key role in the tale. The primary focus of the story, however, centers on metempsychosis. As he did in "Metzengerstein" Poe again uses the notion of the transmigration of souls to frighten his readers. Whereas in his first tale metempsychosis permits a transformed murder victim to exercise vengeance on his killer, here Poe discusses this phenomenon from a slightly different perspective.

Morella has the ability to cheat death. When her corporeal form degenerates she merely enters the frame of her infant daughter and continues her existence. Such a power would appear desirable. Poe, however, creates the impression that for Morella death carries with it none of the peace usually associated with its effects. Possessing a form of immortality, Morella finds little comfort in her ability to exist eternally. Like "Shadow" and "Silence," this tale becomes another treatise on the nature of death. "Morella" has greater affinities with "Silence" than with "Shadow." In the latter, death is presented as a communal condition. The dead, so we are to assume, mingle freely. "Silence," on the other hand, treats death as a form of isolation, something with which the individual must grapple alone. In "Morella," the mysterious woman fails to succumb to death's power but appears separated from all other forms of mortal and immortal life. Becoming what we might call a Wandering Jew, Morella must face the utter loneliness produced by her condition. She finds none of the comfort that eternal rest provides ordinary mortals. Poe shows that if human identity survives after death, it could conceivably exist in a state of infinite, desolate solitude. Once again the reader's fear of death allows Poe to examine all possible contingencies regarding the nature of eternity.

The epigraph to the tale prepares us for the desolation produced by Morella's condition: "Itself, by itself solely, ONE everlastingly, and single" (229). Thus the reader learns of Morella's plight. As the tale proper begins, the narrator remarks that his wife shunned society and studied various works of the occult. Like Egaeus, this speaker also reads such books and finds himself perplexed by the contemplation of infinity. He falls prey to his curiosity, and the joy of studying alongside Morella soon gives way to horror:

> And then--then, when, poring over forbidden pages, I felt a forbidden spirit enkindling within me--would Morella place her cold hand upon my own. . . . And then, hour after hour, would I linger by her side, and dwell upon the music of her voice--until, at length, its melody was tainted with terror,--and there fell a shadow upon my soul--and I grew pale, and shuddered inwardly at those too unearthly tones. And thus, joy suddenly faded into horror, and the most beautiful became the most hideous. . . . (230)

Her husband becomes disturbed by his ever-increasing knowledge of the nature of the beyond. Morella's terror results from her inability to find eternal peace. As the narrator finds himself drawn into further discussions of mortality, his uneasiness heightens. Observing Morella's reservations, he is unable to avoid depression. The ecstasy proffered by Morella borders on terror.[20] Describing their studies, our speaker makes an important revelation concerning "the notion of that identity *which at death is or is not lost forever* . . ." (231). When they examine this topic, Morella's husband notices that she becomes markedly agitated. Her upset results from awareness that her own identity has existed eternally. The future provides no relief from her wanderings.

Overcome by disease, Morella prepares to "die," and knows that she will continue to live once her spiritual essence enters a new body. Her condition worsens to the point where her husband, terrified by the gloom present in his "dying" wife, actually hopes for her death. In order to understand better Morella's lonely pilgrimage, we should look briefly at the first version of the tale in which she sings a "Catholic Hymn." The third stanza describes a truant soul that the Virgin Mary's love guides to heaven. In the concluding stanza, the singer prays for a future amid the presence of Mary and the other heavenly hosts. Morella longs for such a placid existence. For some unknown reason (perhaps her study of occult and forbidden topics), Morella is doomed by the curse of a lonely, infinite existence. When she mutters the words of the hymn, she prays for relief. The hymn, unfortunately, brings her no comforting results. Lying on her "deathbed," Morella tells her husband that his life will become one of unending sorrow. Such uneasiness will result from his growing awareness of Morella's horrible dilemma. Life will no longer prove enjoyable. As she dies, Morella gives birth to a daughter, and Morella's soul apparently now transmigrates from mother to child. At first the narrator strongly loves his little girl. After ten years, however, he faces a horrifying realization:

> day after day did I discover new points of resemblance
> in the child to her mother, the melancholy and the dead.

> And, hourly, grew darker these shadows of similitude,
> and more full, and more definite, and more perplexing,
> and more hideously terrible in their aspect. (234)

After he christens his nameless daughter with the name of his
dead wife, he completes the eternal cycle of Morella's endless
life. Her name seems to have a terrifying life of its own.[21] By
uttering the word, the narrator seems to unleash the power of
some sort of magic spell. We must also recall that in order to
summon a creature from beyond a person must speak that
being's name. Morella's daughter goes to the sepulcher so that
her mother's spirit may take control of a new body. On her
mother's tomb, the young Morella, suddenly colored with the
hues of death, acknowledges the presence of her mother's
essence, a spirit that seeks to re-enter the world of mortals.
When his child dies and he bears her corpse to its last resting
place, the narrator learns that the bones of the elder Morella
have vanished. Laughing the laugh of the enlightened madman
(as do Roderick Usher and the demon in "Silence"), he now
discovers the truth behind Morella's existence. Subsequent visits
to the charnel house would no doubt reveal that Morella,
unable to experience the peaceful sleep of death, still wanders
the earth like a hermit. Using the fear of death and to some
degree the dread of the supernatural, Poe in "Morella" comments on one of the more sinister possibilities of infinity.

   Three years after "Morella," in "Ligeia," Poe treats again the
subject of metempsychosis. One major point, however, differentiates "Ligeia" from its predecessor. The central female character
appears a good deal more cruel than her counterpart in
"Morella." Ligeia resists death by violently seizing the body of
Lady Rowena. Her eternal struggle with mortality leads her to
assume the role of a demon who must enter the corporeal
essence of some unsuspecting human victim. The power of her
will corresponds with those descriptions (found in folklore) of
the psychic commandingness allegedly possessed by vampires or
devils. Whereas Morella passed her life spark to her offspring,

Ligeia searches for helpless bodily hosts. Poe uses his tale to treat further the subject of the afterlife. Terrorizing his readers, he describes the possibility of a malign spirit preying consciously upon human souls. His story also features elements associated with the fears of illness and physical deformity, enclosure, noises, and heights. A tale in which meditation on infinity produces a mixed response of hope and fear,[22] "Ligeia" genuinely terrifies its audience.

Beginning with a typically Poesque epigraph--treating the ability of a strong will to conquer death--the tale quickly shifts to an introduction of the narrator, Ligeia's husband. His description of their early relationship is filled with a sense of foreboding. He recalls that he met her in an old, decaying Rhenish city. Eventually her body will rot and force her to find another physical frame. Ligeia "buries" herself in curious study that "deadens" impressions of the external world. Like Egaeus and Morella, then, she inters herself in a contemplation of infinity (a variation on the premature burial theme then so popular in literature). We should also note that Ligeia possesses high intelligence, stunning beauty, and a hypnotically enticing low voice, all of which link her to demons and vampires who attempt to lure earthly quarry into eternal perdition. The most obvious feature bonding her to the traditional supernatural guest of myth is the entrancing look present in her unusually large, sinister eyes. These orbs arouse a strange sentiment in her husband: "I recognized it . . . sometimes in the survey of a rapidly-growing vine--in the contemplation of a moth, a butterfly, a chrysalis, a stream of running water" (314). All of these phenomena can metamorphose and, to an extent, assume a new form of existence. Perhaps the narrator sees in his wife's eyes, which supposedly serve as gateways to the soul, the ultimate reality behind her mysterious life. Like a demon or vampire, Ligeia would be capable of changing her shape and, consequently, her very being. Her powers will manifest themselves when she later inhabits the body of Rowena. We should also note that her eyes delight and frighten the narrator, again demonstrating

Poe's awareness of the relationship between fear and the sublime.

Describing her physical appearance, the narrator seems to delineate a being undeniably suggestive of traditional vampire lore:

> In stature she was tall, somewhat slender, and, in her latter days, even emaciated. I would in vain attempt to portray the majesty, the quiet ease, of her demeanor, or the incomprehensible lightness and elasticity of her footfall. She came and departed as a shadow. (314)

He later recalls her hair, which he characterizes as not merely black but as "raven black." The reader realizes that such revelations produce an ominous aura. Ligeia's height produces an anxiety in her husband similar to that felt by an observer who looks up at any high object. The "high" knowledge of Ligeia will eventually contribute to her husband's fall from the grasp of reason as he recognizes the strength of her demonic powers.

Extremely passionate, Ligeia exerts a strong influence on her husband, who obviously possesses a will inferior to hers. Her passion resembles strongly that which is associated with demons. Soon, however, her host body grows ill and she must prepare for a temporary departure from her physical existence. Repeating a poem that she had written, Ligeia intensifies the dramatic impact of her will's triumph.[23] One passage in particular, "'Through a circle that ever returneth in/To the self-same spot'" (318), suggests the infinite nature of Ligeia's will.

Upon the "death" of his wife, the distraught husband leaves for England. The abbey he purchases helps to initiate the endless cycle through which Ligeia lives. Described as gloomy and decayed, the building recalls the old, dim city on the Rhine where the speaker first met his wife. Little does he suspect that he is about to encounter her once again. He remarries, now choosing the blonde, blue-eyed Lady Rowena. Their bridal chamber looks like a crypt. The great height and pentagonal shape of the room seem to beckon Ligeia. She appears worthy of a "high" room because of her lofty intelligence, and the pentagram shape represents a device used to communicate with beings in the occult world. The odd decorations present in the chamber imply that the narrator, influenced by Ligeia's teachings, longs for her return. His inability to love Rowena, a wife who feels no affection for her husband, makes him think only of his beloved Ligeia.

With the illness of Rowena comes the second stage in Ligeia's process of rejuvenation. The Lady of Tremaine claims that strange sounds emanate from the dark recesses of her room. Her husband informs us:

> I could not fail to observe a similar increase in the nervous irritation of her temperament, and in her excitability by trivial causes of fear. She spoke again, and now more frequently and pertinaciously, of the sounds . . . and of the unusual motions among the tapestries. . . . (324)

Ligeia has returned to her husband. What now occurs in the tale takes place near the beginning of September, a time associated with falling-off and decay. The ninth month of the year also serves as a fitting background for Ligeia's rebirth. Feeling the presence of an invisible object, the narrator thinks that he sees a shadow on the carpet and hears the gentle fall of a light footstep. Ligeia, at this juncture a pure spirit, cannot be seen because she has not yet entered a body. Soon after these events Rowena takes a drink:

> As Rowena was in the act of raising the wine to her lips, I saw, or may have dreamed that I saw, fall within the goblet, as if from some invisible spring in the atmosphere of the room, three or four large drops of a brilliant and ruby colored fluid. (325)

She soon dies, and her husband prepares her for burial. As he sits in the room with his wife's corpse, he hears a sob come from the bed on which the body lies. Ligeia is gradually entering the body of Rowena. As the narrator's thoughts of his first wife become more frequent and ardent, Rowena's body shows increased signs of life. During this entire process the onlooking husband watches in horror. His fear paralyzes him, and thereafter he can only powerlessly observe the hideous episode unfolding before him. Dumbfounded, he witnesses the body of Rowena change shape and grow taller. Once he sees the black hair and the familiar eyes, however, he knows that Ligeia has assumed control of another victim and returned to life. Her strong will permits her physical characteristics to overpower those of Rowena. The passionate, horrified nature of the narrator's closing remarks contrast markedly with the more emotionally placid conclusion of "Morella." In "Ligeia," Poe uses traditional demon lore and other fears to exploit his reader's uneasiness regarding eternity.[24]

"The Fall of the House of Usher," Poe's most famous tale, has elicited widely divergent critical opinions. Some scholars see the piece as an exploration of the artistic imagination; others view it as one dealing with erotic, sexual interests. Numerous readers believe that Poe concerns himself with the nature of insanity, the scientific explanations behind seemingly supernatural events, or various sociological implications.[25] For the most part, however, "Usher" must be read as Poe's most profound statement on fear. Concentrating on the fears cited by Rush, he plunges deep into the reader's subconscious and slashes it with knife-like words. He employs the misgivings produced by weather and nature, horses and riding, illness, insanity, death, water, the supernatural, and enclosure. The entire tale captures both its characters and its readers and imprisons them in a cage of fearful anxiety. The narrator's remarks in the opening scene concerning the insufferable gloom pervading his spirit, show that no relief is in sight: "I say insufferable; for the feeling was unrelieved by any of that half-pleasurable, because poetic, sentiment, with which the mind usually receives even the sternest natural images of the desolate or terrible" (397). As he informs us a few sentences below, nothing in the story remotely resembles the sublime. Poe experiments, in other words, with the effects of unmitigated terror and fear.

The first sentence strikes immediately at the reader's psychic vulnerabilities. A dark, autumn day seems to possess all the quiet of a tomb. The low clouds enclose the entire scene like the walls of a mausoleum. We learn that the narrator travels alone, separated from the rest of humanity. Gloom wraps itself around him like a shroud. He journeys on horseback. Like Metzengerstein and the narrator in "Tarr and Fether," Roderick's friend rides into a world in which fear will overcome him. When he steps down from his horse he leaves the lofty realm of reason and allows himself to enter the domain of despair. The powerful animal that bears him to his friend carries him into the jaws of a strong adversary--fear. Poe characters who travel on horses rarely enjoy their experience as their steeds usually take them toward some physical or mental destruction. In "Usher" the equestrian-narrator will soon suffer from a psychic depression engendered by fear.

Fear of water plays on the reader's hidden chords of distress when the narrator observes the black, lurid tarn lying close to the bleak mansion. When he gazes into the hellish waters and contemplates the house's reflection, he receives a foreshadowing of the fate that awaits this castle of fear. The tarn, then, will become a watery grave much like that described in "MS. Found." Nature enshrouds the home with the darkness of death. The decayed trees surrounding the building and the fungi growing on the eaves create an odd atmosphere of death that frightens the visitor:

I had so worked upon my imagination really to believe that about the whole mansion and domain there hung an atmosphere peculiar to themselves and their immediate vicinity--an atmosphere which had no affinity with the

air of heaven, but which had reeked up from the
decayed trees, and the gray wall and the silent tarn--a
pestilent and mystic vapour, dull, sluggish, faintly dis-
cernible, and leaden-hued. (399-400)

Contrary to his own speculations, the narrator does not dream
the sights he sees. In this tale nature appears to conspire against
the mansion and its inhabitants. Biding its time, it waits, like a
beast of prey, for the proper moment to devour the decaying
family. Nature, then, becomes a type of demon that longs to
destroy human souls. Once the crack in the building and the
fissure in Usher's sanity grow larger, the trap will spring and
embrace its quarry.

Externally the mansion appears sinister and ill-omened. As
he enters his friend's domicile, the speaker discovers that its
internal decor resembles closely its bleak surroundings. Black
floors, somber tapestries, and high, lofty windows that permit
only faint beams of blood red light to enter the chamber conjure
images of a tomb or prison. Roderick possesses "a cadaverous-
ness of complexion" (401) that indicates he will soon become a
prisoner of death. The narrator-friend learns that Usher's
nervous agitation arises from the influence of "the grim phantasm, FEAR." Roderick believes that his house and its environs
exert a mysterious influence over him. Whether or not this is
the case, Usher *believes* in the legend. Never leaving the sad
mansion, he sinks deeper into the abyss of fear and the insanity
it often produces. Usher becomes a slave to terror and awaits
his destruction.

The physical condition of his ill sister Madeline heightens
Roderick's fear of death. Filled with dread when he observes
her corpse-like body, the narrator learns that she has been
overpowered by some baffling disease: "A settled apathy, a
gradual wasting away of the person, and frequent although
transient affections of a partially cataleptical character were the
unusual diagnosis" (404). His sister's imminent death troubles
Roderick to such an extent that he appears to radiate a

darkness that casts gloom over everything. Painting a picture of an object that resembles a burial vault, Usher grows more depressed with each passing moment. His song "The Haunted Palace" traces his own mental disintegration. The lines from the sixth stanza, "And travellers now within that valley,/ Through the red-litten windows, see/ Vast forms that move fantastically/ To a discordant melody" (407), reflect accurately the reality unfolding before the speaker. Believing in the sentience of all matter, Roderick feels that the very stones that comprise his home create an aura of terror and pain.

After Madeline succumbs to her disease, Roderick decides to place the corpse in a "temporary" tomb. He refuses to bury her in the family burial ground. Following the interment the narrator notices that Usher becomes increasingly terrified, as if he seems oppressed by some horrible secret. Here we must pause and consider the nature of Madeline's malady. Described as cataleptic, she has been afflicted with a disease that makes its sufferers appear dead. The vampire endures a similar existence as it rests during the day prior to emerging from its coffin at night. Might Madeline be a vampire? The speaker first sees her as night approaches; Usher informs him that she has succumbed to the power of her destroyer. Later she breaks out of her tomb *at night*. If she were a vampire she would possess the great strength needed to free herself from the vault. The desolate land around Usher's house resembles that in which the undead usually have their abodes. Upon viewing her earlier in the tale, Usher's companion sustains a stupefaction not unlike the hypnotic trance often used by vampires to subjugate their prey. Aware of his sister's unholy condition, Usher decides to bury her deep below his own house in a tomb that resembles a dungeon. This action alerts the reader that the undead must rest in their native soil. These possibilities suggest Poe's insinuating a supernatural being, an evil creature that assails the Usher family's high estate, into this tale. At the very least, we can conclude that Usher *thinks* that such is the case. Regardless of the "facts" that inspire them, his fears are very real indeed.

Poe makes a curious statement regarding the nature of fear through his narrator's observation of the macabre situation in which Roderick finds himself: "It was no wonder that his condition terrified--that it infected me. I felt creeping upon me, by slow yet certain degrees, the wild influences of his own fantastic yet impressive superstitions" (411). Unable to account logically for his horrible feelings, Usher's companion discovers the contagious nature of fear. Poe shows how the germs of fear prove immune to any resistance mounted by the victim. When the narrator reads the "Mad Trist" and tries to bring relief to Usher, he learns that at times no measure of literary fear can conquer the demons that pollute the mind. The reader might suspect that by means of this story within a story Poe warns his audience that "Usher" provides no shelter from fear's power.

Roderick is affected by the unearthly sounds that echo those found in the tale of Launcelot Canning. The fierce storm raging outside shows that nature prepares to swallow its deranged victim. Noticing the "life-like" characteristics of the wind, the narrator experiences what Usher referred to earlier as the sentience of nature. Benjamin Rush and later psychologists note that the person faced with fear will freeze or run. During Madeline's ghastly return Roderick remains paralyzed by fear. The speaker, on the other hand, flees the mansion in terror. At this point he notices a "wild light" similar to that appearing in the conclusion of "Metzengerstein." Growing wider, the crack in the house causes the collapse of the once proud family estate. Nature seems to rejoice as the narrator notices that "there was a long tumultuous shouting sound like the voice of a thousand waters--and the deep and dank tarn at my feet closed sullenly and silently over the fragments of the '*House of Usher*'" (417). This concluding image suggests the idea of a gravedigger, nature, quietly shoveling dirt into a new grave. The tumult of the cataclysmic scene gives way to a silence associated with death as the heavens enclose the mansion in a watery sepulcher.

Although the narrator flees for his life, Poe's tale offers no real sanctuary for the reader seeking to avoid the terror of fear.

In stories like "MS. Found," "The Pit and the Pendulum," and "A Descent into the Maelström," Poe's protagonists are freed from fear's grasp by means of spiritual rejuvenation. "Usher," however, provides no escape for its hero or audience.[26] Battering his reader's subconscious with a carefully wrought formula, Poe presents a terrifying picture in which fear roams unrestrained. No salvation exists.

"William Wilson" discusses another of the national fears that plagued the American psyche during the early and mid-nineteenth century. At the time people feared that the lust for material wealth would corrupt America from within. The desire to attain large amounts of money might erode the mores of otherwise upstanding citizens. As the country continued to expand its physical boundaries, its inhabitants saw the opportunity for increased personal profit. In this tale Poe illustrates the consequences that befall a young man who ruthlessly pursues the demon of wealth. Despite a middle-class upbringing, Wilson develops arrogant and aristocratic tastes and exploits the weaknesses of others. Although he fails to mount the proverbial soapbox, Poe does create a story in which he confirms one of the darkest fears present in the minds of those thinkers who pondered America's future. He also adds to the overall effect by using traditional psychological fears.

The opening paragraphs create the impression that Wilson is in the act of making a deathbed confession. Reprimanding himself, he speaks of the terrible misery and the despicable crimes he perpetrated: "From me, in an instant all virtue dropped bodily as a mantle" (426). As death approaches he feels that it brings a welcome peace that he never experienced during life. Yet he also believes that dismal, limitless clouds stand between himself and heaven. Without mentioning the specific cause of his misery, Wilson appears to warn his fellows:

> I would have them allow--what they cannot refrain from allowing--that, although temptation may have ere-while existed as great, man was never *thus*, at least, tempted

before--certainly, never *thus* fell. And is it therefore that
he has never thus suffered? Have I not indeed been
living in a dream? And am I not now dying a victim to
the horror and the mystery of the wildest of all subluna-
ry visions? (427)

We eventually learn that his passionate desire to amass personal
wealth creates for him a hell on earth. Early in life Wilson
becomes "self-willed." His problem, then, began in childhood. As
he grows older he exercises freely the whims of his will without
tempering his cravings with the wise counsel of conscience.

Wilson's education, in a curious way, seems to have nurtured
his evil propensities. The English school he attended was
situated in a gloomy, misty country village. Besides engulfing the
town, the mist clouds Wilson's young mind and prohibits him
from recognizing the dark leanings of his thoughts. Gnarled
trees, shadowed avenues, and the still, dusky atmosphere create
a typically Gothic setting that embraces its victim in a strangle-
hold. The schoolhouse itself is surrounded by a high brick wall
topped with mortar and broken glass: "This prison-like rampart
formed the limit of our domain" (428). Unable to maintain a
healthy contact with the outside world, Wilson's corrupting
thoughts thrive and further isolate him from his conscience. His
statement that images of his old school provide him with
temporary relief from his sufferings proves ironic. If anything,
his being "walled up" from normal interaction with the external
world increased the severity of his malady. Even his schoolroom,
with its long, narrow, and unusually low ceiling assumes the
appearance of a coffin. Traditional death imagery foreshadows
the subsequent demise of his moral faculty.

Describing his years at school, Wilson admits that his mind
developed uncommonly and pursued the *outré*. He embraces the
spirit of the age when he cites Voltaire: "*Oh, le bon temps, que
ce siècle de fer!*" ["Oh, what a good time it was, that age of
iron!"] (431). Again, Poe's irony is clear. When he encounters
the second William Wilson, the personification of conscience,

Wilson feels that this odd visitor attempts constantly to thwart or mortify him. Here Poe relies on the belief that any man who sees his double will soon die.[27] Altering slightly this superstition, Poe has his character live while his ability to act morally yields to Wilson's wild passions.

When he describes his years at Eaton and Oxford, Wilson reveals the specific nature of his weakness. Although they did not belong to the aristocracy, Wilson's parents possessed enough money to send their son to exclusive schools and provide him with an annuity:

> Thither I soon went, the uncalculating vanity of my parents furnishing me with an outfit and annual establishment, which would enable me to indulge at will in the luxury already so dear to my heart--to vie in profuseness of expenditure with the haughtiest heirs of the wealthiest earldoms in Great Britain. (440)

Wine, gambling, and what Wilson calls "more dangerous seductions" become his trademarks as he proceeds down the road of vice. He takes advantage of friends as he seeks to increase his income at their expense. Using a rigged card game to rob his wealthy associate Glendinning of a fortune, Wilson grows terrified as the chamber doors suddenly burst open and all the candles blow out. Here at the height of Wilson's deception enters his double, shrouded in a nearly supernatural darkness, to reveal Wilson's chicanery. Poe adds the Gothic device of an unearthly visitor to intensify the horror inherent in Wilson's situation. Leaving for the Continent in shame, Wilson cannot run from himself: "*I fled in vain.* My evil destiny pursued me as if in exultation, and proved, indeed, that the exercise of its mysterious dominion had as yet only begun" (444-445).

Frustrated continually by conscience, Wilson becomes enraged. His cupidity has led him into the realms of other related passions such as ambition, vengeance, and lust. As the second Wilson foils him, Wilson's fears increase to the point where he decides to kill his opponent. Now he is beyond hope. Greed leads him to perform an act that will result in complete moral death. Attempting to seduce Di Broglio's beautiful wife, Wilson is interrupted by his double. After he stabs his adversary, a mirror mysteriously appears and Wilson, petrified with terror, observes his own pale, blood-covered image. The vision in the glass turns out to be that of his conscience-double. Such an action is fitting because by destroying his enemy Wilson has forfeited his soul. Like the vampire, he now casts no reflection in the mirror. By conquering his foe, Wilson has lost any chance of achieving happiness on earth or in heaven. He will remain a slave to the vices resulting from his craving for wealth. Wilson seeks financial strength but gains instead a moral weakness that proves fatal. Conscious of the forces that threatened to destroy America, Poe uses his tale to depict the malignant consequences of humanity's efforts to achieve profuse wealth. Capital interests must mingle with moral responsibility if society intends to survive.

"A DESCENT INTO THE MAELSTRÖM," "ELEONORA," "THE MASQUE OF THE RED DEATH," "THE PIT AND THE PENDULUM," "THE TELL-TALE HEART," AND "THE BLACK CAT"

Poe sets "A Descent into the Maelström" in a particularly dangerous part of the sea, a frightening whirlpool off the Norwegian coast. A story of nautical adventure, "A Descent" closely resembles the earlier "MS. Found," although one crucial element differentiates the two pieces. In "A Descent," the principal character survives his ordeal. The sailor experiences the harshness of nature, but through rational thought he endures his watery trial. Similar to "Shadow" and "Silence," "MS. Found" and "A Descent" present the alternatives evident in a given situation. Poe balances the notions of death and life on his fictional scales. Realizing that hope and despair mingle freely in life, he examines the conflicting nature of being. Whereas "MS. Found" merely hints its narrator's spiritual rejuvenation, "A Descent" brings the idea to its fruition. Changed by his harrowing voyage, the Norwegian sailor, like Coleridge's ancient mariner, hopes that others may benefit from his unpleasant visions. His sense of the beauty of the maelstrom saves him from destruction.[28] This tale, in many respects, typifies Poe's fiction of fear. The fears of water, sounds, burial, nature, heights, depths, open spaces, and riding evident in the sketch show that Poe employs dread to attract an audience. Despite the strength of such reservations, an individual can overpower them by relying on his ability to assess his predicament. Like the sailor, the reader, altered somewhat by his encounter with acute mental stress, can emerge a bit wiser. As he does in many other tales, Poe in "A Descent" toys with his reader's response to fear and provides him with an anodyne for the fright rooted in the mind. The horrors scattered along the road to the mastery of dread show, in the words of the epigraph, that "the ways of God in Nature, as in Providence, are not as *our* ways . . ." (577). There can be no redemption without pain.

Mental distress arises in the opening paragraphs as Poe incorporates the fear of heights into his tale. Anxious to relate his story to the young visitor, the sailor takes his companion to the summit of a high peak overlooking a sinister expanse of water. Reacting to the crag's great height, the young man finds himself shaken by the old man's proximity to the precipice:

> In truth so deeply was I excited by the perilous position of my companion, that I fell at full length upon the ground, clung to the shrubs around me, and dared not even glance upward at the sky--while I struggled in vain to divest myself of the idea that the very foundations of

the mountain were in danger from the fury of the winds. (578)

Many people find themselves affected similarly when they stand atop a high object. Here Poe relates accurately the typical human reaction to great height. We must also notice that the speaker is upset not merely by his own feelings but by the state of the old sailor, who had earlier admitted that the great height makes him giddy. Poe reveals the contagious nature of fear and shows how one's plight might easily influence another. Most readers, reacting in a manner similar to that of the young narrator, mentally cling to the solid ground beneath them as they observe this scene. Reader *and* protagonist grow dizzy, thus assuring Poe of keeping his characters and audience firmly in his grasp.

Toward the conclusion of this episode Poe provides a hint that might help one minimize the power of fear. Describing his own uneasiness, the speaker comments: "It was long before I could *reason* [my italics] myself into sufficient courage to sit up and look out into the distance" (578). Here we have a possible solution to the dilemma of dread. Rational thought provides the means through which human beings can conquer their psychic misgivings. Reason allows the young man to overcome his fear, just as it permitted the sailor to survive his hellish adventure. The lofty summit from which this tale unfolds represents the "high" knowledge that the sailor gains through his brush with death. He hopes to pass some of his insight into the mind of his listener.

Viewing the picture around him, the young man is disturbed by the black cliffs, the gloomy surf, and the howling water. Seemingly limitless, the vast expanse of ocean becomes an open, desolate space that extends as far as the eye can see. Fear of open spaces troubles the gentleman as he contemplates this endless prairie of water. Moaning and growling, the sea resembles a ravenous wolf that longs for its victim's blood; sounds arising from the numerous waves suggest a pack of predatory animals. All nature seems bent on the destruction of any unsuspecting sailors. Poe cleverly uses sound to terrify his characters and readers.

A few minutes later the young man notices that the tumultuous scene seems to have transformed itself into a peaceful, glass-like pond. Whirlpools have grown calm. Much to his amazement, however, the sea suddenly reverts to its original fury with an intensity not before evident. The sailor, possessing an intelligence imparted by the sea, cautions: "But these intervals of tranquility are only at the turn of the ebb and flood, and in calm weather, and last but a quarter of an hour, its violence gradually returning" (581). Although he speaks directly about the horrifying maelstrom, the sailor seems to comment on the power of fear itself. Just when a person believes that he has conquered this emotion, it returns more powerful than ever. Like the whirlpool, fear appears a part of nature that strikes relentlessly at the mind. Even the sailor, who has avoided its grasp and survived his shipwreck, still admits to being frightened by a shadow. The old man has mastered the spectre but cannot destroy it. If fear has been reduced from the level of demon it has become a lesser devil, a poltergeist determined to produce as much mischief as it can. Perhaps this message forms the core of the sailor's remarks to his associate: individual battles can be won, but winning the war is altogether another matter. Despite numerous setbacks fear still exists.

Whereas fear terrifies it also proves attractive. Aware of this fact, Poe relies on the concept of the sublime in "A Descent." Contemplating the horror of the surging sea, the young man recognizes in it a certain magnificence. He remarks that the maelstrom radiates an irresistible "deadly attraction." Later, the old sailor admits: "'Never shall I forget the sensation of awe, horror, and admiration with which I gazed about me'" (590). He and his brothers willfully risked their lives when they navigated the tempestuous waters. Various fears assailed them. Tossed about by the force of the watery abyss, their vessel becomes a wild, uncontrollable animal that they must ride toward a nautical grave. Captured by the cruel ocean, the sailors fall from the water's surface into the depths of darkness: "And then down we came with a sweep, a slide, and a plunge, that made me feel sick and dizzy, as if I was falling from some lofty mountain-top . . ." (587). This passage suggests the image with which the tale opens. Here the fear of heights and depths is realized as the ship plunges into the chasm. Darkness buries the men and they become entombed. All bear the pallor of death. The grotesque sounds emanating from the watery pit engender spasms of terror. Locked in the jaws of the gulf, the old sailor comes to an awareness that provides him with a means of escape:

> "It may look like boasting--but what I tell you is truth--I began to reflect how magnificent a thing it was to die in such a manner, and how foolish it was in me to think of so paltry a consideration as my own individual life, in view of so wonderful a manifestation of God's power." (588)

Having overcome the power of fear, the sailor can view his situation rationally. Freed from his misgivings he sees the beauty present around him. His brothers go insane because of inabilities to subdue their fears. The ship's lone survivor prays to God and soon learns how to free himself. His earlier terrors are replaced by a natural curiosity. Horror becomes hope, symbolized by the beautiful rainbow he sees. Clinging to a barrel (its circular shape suggests infinity) he resists the pull of the whirlpool and soon emerges on the surface of the sea.

As the tale concludes, the sailor confesses that once the immediate danger was removed he again fell prey to fear. Poe implies that thinking about dread or observing a person who has succumbed to this emotion produces a more intense state of excitement than actually encountering a stressful situation. After his rescue, the sailor recalls his adventure and allows fear to master reason. His altered physical appearance coincides with Benjamin Rush's description of fear's effects.[29] Unfortunately, his mind has also been altered by his unpleasant experience when he remembers the horrors that he confronted. Hoping to kindle similar reactions in the members of his audience, Poe strives to force their hidden fears to the surface so that, like the sailor in "A Descent," they will explore eagerly their own mental whirlpools.

In "Eleonora" Poe relies on the "returning woman" motif to terrify his readers. A close examination of early and late versions of this work reveals that, like Morella and Ligeia, Eleonora possesses the ability to live eternally.[30] Yet the reader must wonder why Poe deleted certain passages that appeared in the *Gift* text of 1842 when he revised the tale for subsequent publication. The original piece suggests strongly that Eleonora returns to her lover (the narrator) in the form of the beautiful Ermengarde. When we consider Poe's cuts, however, we see that the tale becomes a good deal more ambiguous. Images of earthly happiness mingle with representations of ominous gloom and present a most puzzling portrait of human affection. Unlike Poe's other tales of "love," "Eleonora" ends happily. The narrator experiences a bliss rarely felt by the typical Poe protagonist. Perhaps Poe's changes demonstrate a desire to avoid the repetition that would arise from his use of a plot similar to those of his earlier tales of mysterious women. On the other hand, the story's nebulousness may result from the author's editorial carelessness. The truth lying at the bottom of this literary well most likely indicates that Poe intended the work to be ambiguous, just as life itself often proves difficult to interpret. Conflicting emotions besiege the human heart. As we shall see, the happy Valley of the Many-Coloured Grass is tinted with many fearful shades.

Poe's epigraph, "*Sub conversatione formae specificae salva anima*" ["Under the protection of a specific form, the soul is safe."] (638), indicates that spiritual and physical rejuvenation plays a key role in the story. Describing his current state of mind, the narrator speculates that men who ponder the nature of infinity "obtain glimpses of eternity, and thrill . . . to find that they have been upon the verge of the great secret" (638). The reader must decide whether the speaker has become mad or actually encountered the secret of eternal life. Traditional beliefs hold that madmen often perceive the truth of the universe. The speaker tells us that he finds himself overcome by shadow and doubt whenever he thinks of the period following Eleonora's death. Subsequent actions place the reader in a similar condition.

Conflicting images permeate Poe's description of the odd valley. Hills surround the region and shut out sunlight. A certain unnatural light, therefore, colors the entire scene. Thousands of trees embower this magic land and cast darkness over it, yet numerous beautiful flowers abound. The reader feels as if the valley itself becomes a type of grave, encircled by the walls of earth formed by the many hills. Perhaps the flowers are similar to those used at funerals. This idea is supported by the ruby red asphodel that grows along with the buttercups, daisies, and violets. Writers often associate the asphodel with death. Here we should note a curious description of Eleonora appearing only in the *Gift* version. Closely resembling Ligeia, Eleonora walks so lightly that she does not trample the asphodels when she steps upon them. Poe thus suggests that this lady circumvents death and manages to avoid its embrace. All versions of the tale mention her luminous eyes. Their lustre mirrors that of a bright burning soul that glows with the fire of immortality.

Death imagery, however, continues to trouble the reader. Fantastic trees grow in this valley. They resemble serpents, and the audience suspects that Poe creates a nature similar to that in Eden. These trees grow virtually sideways as they seek the light that creeps into the center of the valley only at noon. We must conclude that much of this mysterious land, for the greater part of the day, is bathed in darkness. Visions of serpents and blackness allow Poe to rely on traditional fear. Nature assumes a sinister aspect when it sends a huge cloud over the basin. This fog "sank, day by day, lower and lower, until its edges rested upon the tops of the mountains, turning all their dimness into magnificence, and shutting us up, as if forever, within a magic prison-house of grandeur and of glory" (641). The happy lovers, experiencing a sublime sense of elation, are entombed in a world of eclipsed pleasure. Originating in the region of Hesper, the Evening Star, the cloud symbolizes the eternal evening toward which all creation moves. Once the passion of the two lovers increases, so does the number of asphodels. Death looms large as Eleonora grows ill. Her greatest fear concerning death is that once she has died the speaker will fall in love with a woman of "the outer and every-day world" (642). Her lover assures her that he will never love a maiden of earth. These remarks show that Poe intends Eleonora to be a creature from the realm of eternity. Her promise to return to her cousin, either directly or through some sorts of heavenly sounds, reinforces this notion. After she dies, "life" leaves the valley. Nevertheless, although the speaker becomes distraught, he sees that the asphodels wither. We thus receive another hint concerning Eleonora's power over finitude. When she later comes back to her lover she conquers death. Currently unaware of his beloved's strength, he leaves his homeland a dejected man.

At this point we need to examine carefully the possibility of Eleonora and Ermengarde being the same person. Eleonora has kept part of her promise by various indications of her spiritual presence. Once these manifestations cease, Ermengarde enters the speaker's life. Is this appearance merely a coincidence? The reader should recall that the narrator earlier described Eleonora as one of the seraphim. He later calls Ermengarde a seraph and a divine angel. She assumes an ethereal quality, just as Eleonora did in the first version. Initially Poe included a scene in which the protagonist notices that Ermengarde bears a strong physical and behavioral resemblance to his dead Eleonora. Later variants contain a passage critical for the reader hoping to penetrate Poe's intention. The speaker remarks "as I looked down into the depths of her memorial eyes I thought only of them--and *of her*" (644). The ambiguity of the italicized words implies that he may be thinking of his beloved Eleonora. The eyes are "memorial" in that they allow him to remember his one true love. More than anything else, however, these eyes *are* those of Eleonora because she has returned to earth. Death permitted her to leave the tomb-like valley and enter the world of reality. When he once again hears Eleonora's voice floating on the night breeze the narrator does not recoil in terror like the men in "Morella" and "Ligeia." Instead he sleeps that sleep of peaceful love. Although second lovers usually bring horror to Poe's male characters,[31] Ermengarde comforts her companion because she is the reincarnated Eleonora. By falling in love with this new woman the protagonist has managed to keep his promise. Once he enters heaven he will learn of love's true power. Death eventually captures all humans, but its strength can be minimized by love.

"Eleonora," then, contains descriptions that play on the reader's fear of nature, darkness, animals, and death. Along with these sinister symbols exist images of eternal love and heavenly happiness. Not a traditional Poe fear sketch, the tale is an attempt to illustrate both sides of a universal human dilemma. Despite its un-Poesque "happy" ending, "Eleonora" serves as a discussion of the many mental reservations arising from the consideration of man's plight.

In "The Masque of the Red Death" Poe returns to the subject of painful death. As he does in "Silence" and "Usher," he provides no relief for his audience. Death's power reigns supreme in this story. Try as they might, Prince Prospero and his associates fail to avoid destruction. Taking advantage of the reservations produced by death, disease, strangers, enclosure, darkness, and the supernatural, Poe produces a piece intended to terrify its readers.

The opening sentences play immediately on the nineteenth-century reader's dread of disease. Like "Shadow," "Masque" begins with a prospect that brings horror to the minds of the public. Although the pestilence Poe describes is chiefly of his own invention, its symptoms are those generally associated with most types of plague:

> There were sharp pains, and sudden dizziness, and then profuse bleeding at the pores, with dissolution. The scarlet stains upon the body and especially upon the face of the victim, were the pest ban which shut him out from the aid and from the sympathy of his fellow-men. (670)

The characteristics of this disease coincide with the effects wrought by mental derangement on the body.[32] Poe's familiarity with the work of Benjamin Rush makes him aware of the physician's belief that intense emotions may create painful physical consequences. Fear, then, is fully capable of producing disease-like results. In addition to suffering from an actual bodily malady the characters in this tale find themselves contaminated with a dread that weakens their resistance. Poe cleverly hints that the illness has two more particularly upsetting symptoms. As the disease spreads it mutilates its victim's face. In a sense the sufferer loses his identity and becomes a misshapen zombie. Here Poe relies on the misgivings produced by the contemplation of physical deformity. The result of this transformation is that the victim becomes "shut out" from his fellow men and enclosed by the darkness of his own pain and the brisk death it produces. Such psychological pressure points no doubt upset and intrigued Poe's readers.

Prospero and his friends decide to flee the ravages of the horrible plague and secure themselves within the Prince's abbey. What they hope will serve as a pleasure-filled isolation ward, however, looks more like Death's domicile. The structure is surrounded by a high wall and secured by means of iron gates. Filled with provisions, the castle resembles an ancient Egyptian tomb, and the revelers seem to possess all they will need to enjoy life--*and* the afterlife. Commenting on the rooms of this

"sanctuary," Poe remarks that "the apartments were so irregular-
ly disposed that the vision embraced but little more than one at
a time" (671). This image suggests catacombs. These seven
chambers connote the seven ages of man from the blue of the
dawn of life to the black night of death.[33] The seventh and
western-most room, decorated with black tapestries and a black
carpet, will become the vault of death at the conclusion of the
tale. Unlike the other apartments, this one has no windows that
correspond to its color; the panes are blood red. These red
windows and the various ornaments scattered about suggest the
sense of death and disorder that envelops the melancholy house
of Roderick Usher. Like Usher's mansion, Prospero's castle will
become a citadel of death.

The ominous ebony clock in the black chamber represents
the passing of time and the gradual destruction of life. As it
records the hour, it terrifies the Prince's guests: "and, while the
chimes of the clock yet rang, it was observed that the giddiest
grew pale, and the more aged and sedate passed their hands
over their brows as if in confused revery or meditation" (672-
673). Hearing the clock toll, the revellers are uncertain whether
they should rejoice or repent. Many probably feel that their
attempts to elude death's grasp are merely temporary and futile.
With each tick of the clock the musicians and waltzers grow
increasingly uneasy. The black chamber with its blood-tinted
windows and ebony timepiece terrifies them and represents the
death that they are striving so much to avoid.

Poe suggests that the people in Prospero's abbey are mad
with fear:

> There were delirious fancies such as the madman fash-
> ions. There were much of the beautiful, much of the
> wanton, much of the *bizarre*, something of the terrible,
> and not a little of that which might have excited disgust.
> (673)

This passage shows how the characters' emotional condition progresses toward a horrible realization of their predicament. Each time the clock strikes, fear creeps deeper into the minds of the revellers. They continue to celebrate but cannot shake the fetters of dread. With the arrival of midnight comes a pensive atmosphere not previously evident. The witching hour also introduces Prospero and his fellows to a strange masked figure who brings with him terror, horror, and revulsion:

> There are chords in the hearts of the most reckless which cannot be touched without emotion. Even with the utterly lost, to whom life and death are equally jests, there are matters of which no jest can be made. . . . The figure was tall and gaunt, and shrouded from head to foot in the habiliments of the grave. (675)

Poe uses the dread of strangers, disease, and death in this episode to upset his readers. The supernatural figure who has suddenly materialized amid the care-free assembly resembles a blood-strewn corpse. None of the individuals who now behold this uninvited guest can manage to see any levity in his presence. Even Prospero shudders with terror and distaste. Eventually he challenges this spectre to identify himself and explain why he has interrupted the merry proceedings. Remaining silent, the visitor moves toward the black chamber. Prospero and his courtiers stand in the blue room when they first encounter the intruder. At this point in the story the spark of life and vitality still glows within these people. Once the ghostly figure moves in the direction of the ebony quarter of the castle, however, the Prince and his retinue follow and progress closer to the death that awaits them. Reaching the extremity of the black room, Prospero attempts to stab the death-like apparition and falls dead himself. Now the other revellers seek to subdue this horrible mummer. They fail to realize that as they rush into the black apartment they are hurrying into the land of death.

Standing in the shadow of the ebony clock, the tall, motionless
being disintegrates as the crowd attempts to seize it. Here Poe
states that humans can never grasp or conquer death. The Grim
Reaper, on the other hand, overpowers all who would destroy
him. One by one the revellers die, "And Darkness and Decay
and the Red Death held illimitable dominion over all" (677).
Poe's capitalization in the concluding sentence intensifies the
belief that like some form of sinister deity, death is the true
master of the universe.

In "Masque," then, Poe presents an idea similar to that
which appears in such tales as "Silence" and "Usher." All human
attempts to thwart death prove futile. No relief emerges in this
sketch. Images of darkness and the grave heighten the macabre
message. A careful craftsman, Poe realizes that occasional doses
of unassuaged horror and fear not only frighten a reader but
also captivate him. Poe uses his literary torch to enlighten the
dark recesses of psychic anxiety.

"The Pit and the Pendulum" contrasts with "Masque" in that
it demonstrates the ability of rational thought to transcend the
fear produced by intense suffering. Although readers might
conclude that Poe is recording the process of disintegration,[34]
he actually describes how the speaker in the tale achieves
salvation through the complete command of his mental faculties.
Despite the fears that attack him, he refuses to yield to the
demon who threatens his very existence. In this piece, then, Poe
states that intense dread can at times be mastered.

As the story begins we learn that the protagonist is a
physically and mentally drained prisoner of the Inquisition who
longs for the serenity of death. He calls himself a sick man who
suffers from intense agony and deadly nausea. Weakened by his
poor bodily condition, his mind alternately perceives his judges
as saviors and then as hostile specters. Standing before his
accusers, he is surrounded by black draperies (of which, as we
now know, Poe is quite fond) and seven tall candles. The
number seven suggests the companions in "Shadow" and the
rooms present in Prospero's abbey. All elements appear to

conspire against the prisoner. Once the speaker swoons, Poe describes his state in a manner suggesting the fear produced by darkness or enclosure: "Then silence, and stillness, and night were the universe" (682). Poe's lengthy first paragraph concludes with a feeling of immense despair and hopelessness.

Recalling his previous semiconscious state, the narrator indicates that his mind has not been permanently impaired by his trying experience: "Yet all was not lost. . . . Even in the grave all *is not* lost. Else there is no immortality for man" (682). His awareness of spiritual reality permits his mind to assay his deplorable situation. He discovers the presence of the hope amid despair that gradually leads him to salvation.[35] Coherent thought will deliver him from the grasp of his tormentors.

Intense suffering must precede redemption, however. Poe's prisoner remembers that ghastly figures resembling supernatural beings carried him into the depths of a gruesome dungeon. This hideous descent troubles the speaker just as a similar downward movement upsets the central characters in "MS. Found" and "A Descent." When he recovers his senses the speaker tells us that he fears to open his eyes: "It was not that I feared to look upon things horrible, but that I grew aghast lest there should be *nothing* to see" (684). His misgivings arise from his reluctance to observe a state identical to that of a dark grave. Feeling surrounded by an eternal blackness and an unbearably close atmosphere he thrusts his arms wildly about him and reveals that he "felt nothing; yet dreaded to move a step, lest I should be impeded by the walls of a *tomb.* Perspiration burst from every pore, and stood in cold beads upon my forehead" (685). Here Poe accurately describes the mental and physical effects of extreme dread. Like all other human beings, the prisoner fears the confines of the tomb. Reacting physically to his condition, and in a manner that recalls Benjamin Rush, he breaks out in a cold sweat. Poe masterfully records the human reaction to fear.

The narrator soon after falls near the brink of a great pit. Once again the horror produced by excessive depth comes into play when he drops a fragment of masonry into the abyss. The noises echoing from the recesses of the chasm frighten the man as does the sound of the door through which his torturers momentarily observe his plight. Eventually the Inquisition's victim trembles at the sound of his own voice. He realizes that his captors have decided to torment him with the prospect of a slow, horrible, psychologically debilitating death.

Awakening from a deep sleep, the narrator is surprised to see that his cell, heretofore dark, has suddenly been illuminated by "a wild, sulphurous lustre" (688). Such sinister light suggests images of hell with its traditional fire and brimstone. Figures of fiends decorate the walls. He now views the dungeon that he previously explored in death-like darkness. Unfortunately, the speaker is currently bound to a wood framework, high above which hangs a huge, menacing pendulum. The narrator curiously admits: "I watched it for some minutes, somewhat in fear, but more in wonder" (689). Again Poe incorporates the sublime into one of his tales. The cruel blade hisses as it descends, and the prisoner also notices some huge rats that crawl about the slimy floor. Poe takes advantage of the human fear of sounds and rodents. In addition, he uses the dread of surgery in his story once he makes it clear that the pendulum will "cut" its helpless victim. The downward velocity of this torture instrument creates a shriek that the narrator believes echoes that of a hellish spirit or a deadly tiger. Despite his acute suffering, Poe's protagonist still feels the fire of hope burning within him. He eventually thinks of a plan that should free him from the path of the huge crescent-shaped scalpel. Mastering the fear of rats, he smears scraps of meat onto the cord securing him to his table so that the disgusting creatures might free him. His plan succeeds, but he must now face a more terrible horror.

Standing in his cell, the prisoner sees that the iron walls glow with the heat of a hellish fire. Dread of the evil eye manifests itself when he learns that "Demon eyes, of a wild and ghastly vivacity, glared upon me in a thousand directions, where none had been visible before . . ." (695). His opponents hope to use the heated walls of the prison to force him into the pit. As the room shrinks and threatens to enclose him in a fiery tomb he moves closer to the gaping gulf. On the verge of destruction, the prisoner screams and suddenly finds himself saved by General Lasalle. The outstretched hand of the Frenchman prevents the narrator from falling prey to his demonic captors. Poe casts this passage such that the General, reaching down from a position of height, assumes the role of God. The conclusion leaves us with the impression that the protagonist's hope and belief in the spiritual immortality of man bring him the ultimate reward of heaven--salvation. In "Pit" Poe shows that man possesses the power to free himself from the embrace of intense fear. Rational thought combined with spiritual awareness assists the man to master his reservations. In this tale Poe demonstrates that man's unique ability to think often saves him from terrifying consequences. The tale, therefore, reinforces the belief in human strength.

"The Tell-Tale Heart" must be considered a treatise on the nature of insanity and the harmful emotions it produces. The horrible actions presented in the story arise from the narrator's demented mind. He suffers from fears that transform him into a warped criminal. In this piece Poe shows how fear often creates demonic effects.

As the tale opens we meet a narrator who goes to great pains to downplay his insanity and prove that his is a healthy mind. When he reveals that he has been afflicted with a "disease," however, his profession of sanity becomes immediately suspect. He later comments: "I heard all things in the heaven and in the earth. I heard many things in hell. How, then, am I mad?" (792). Seemingly possessing stronger affinities with the underworld than with heaven, the speaker appears to have established a rapport with the creatures of darkness. The more he tells us about himself, the more we believe that he *is* insane. Poe's entire first paragraph proves ironic. Early in the tale Poe uses the dread of mental disease and the supernatural to set the stage for the horrors that appear later in the work.

The troubled speaker soon reveals that he was greatly affected by one of the old man's eyes:

> I think it was his eye! yes, it was this! One of his eyes resembled that of a vulture--a pale blue eye, with a film over it. Whenever it fell upon me, my blood ran cold; and so by degrees--very gradually--I made up my mind to take the life of the old man, and thus rid myself of the eye forever. (792)

Fear of the evil eye plays an important role in this tale. Many mentally healthy individuals feel that "the idea of an all-seeing eye, peering at one, even during one's most secret moments, is indeed disturbing."[36] A person afflicted by a form of mental instability would find such an eye even more upsetting. Yet here we must ask ourselves why the speaker fears this mysterious orb. As the organ of sight, the eye perceives all around it. Might not the old man's blue eye be able to unearth some dark, sinister secret concerning the narrator? If we recall the protagonist's state of mind we could conclude that in all likelihood he may have performed previous murders. Overcome by guilt, the speaker believes that perhaps the old man's eye can peer into the reality that lies buried in his soul. In a sense, then, the eye possesses the all-powerful sight of God. Like Satan, the narrator attempts to overpower omnipotence by destroying his foe. He views his antagonist as a demon who must be eliminated. His diseased mind makes him call out his victim's name much as one utters the name of a devil in order to summon him. Calling our attention to his carefully thought-out plan for the old man's destruction, the narrator produces this scheme as proof of his sanity. The reader should note Rush's statement that the madman often possesses a savage cunning that disarms people around him.[37] Despite the speaker's claim to sanity, Poe's readers are aware of his actual mental state.

Fear infects not only the reader and the narrator but the old man as well. We learn that he seems rather wealthy. His room, surrounded by closed shutters, is bathed in a darkness resulting from his dread of robbers. This gloomy chamber will soon become a charnel house. As the protagonist peers into the old man's room, he informs us that his intended victim "was still sitting up in the bed, listening;--just as I have done, night after night, hearkening to the death-watches in the wall" (794). Besides fearing the possible loss of some of his fortune, the old man, like the speaker, dreads the menace of death. The night brings no relief for the owner of the vulture eye and he groans in terror:

> His fears had been . . . growing upon him. He had been trying to fancy them causeless, but could not. . . . Yes, he had found all in vain. *All in vain*; because Death, in approaching him, had stalked with his black shadow before him, and enveloped the victim. (794)

The darkness of death surrounds the old man and will soon enclose him in its grasp. Entering the chamber, the speaker hears the loud beating of the man's terror-stricken heart. Murdering his victim, he surgically dismembers the corpse and buries it in a dark crypt beneath the bedroom's floorboards. He now believes that his fears are behind him; the vulture eye will no longer trouble him. When the police officers visit his home, however, he becomes disturbed by what he imagines is the continual beating of the dead man's heart. Poe again implies that sounds often produce anxiety. The old man's shriek brought the constables to the house, and the noise of the pulsating heart will soon condemn the murderer. Whether or not the narrator actually hears the heartbeat or imagines that sound is not important. The fear resulting from his guilt proves real and drives him to reveal his heinous crime. Poe relies on the misgivings produced by insanity, the supernatural, death, certain loud sounds, surgery, darkness, and enclosure to terrify his audience with the actions of a diseased mind.

Terror and fear play central roles in Poe's "The Black Cat." Like the narrator in "The Tell-Tale Heart," the speaker in this story attempts to convince his listener that he is not mad. Making his statements on the eve of his execution, Poe's protagonist confesses willfully his past misdeeds in order to cleanse his soul. What he has learned from his bizarre experience deals with the presence of evil in the world.[38] Poe reveals that even docile individuals often find themselves slaves of the hostile forces that harass humanity. The dread of certain animals, the supernatural, surgery, the evil eye, enclosure, and sound allow Poe to explore still farther the darker regions of the psyche.

Recalling his horrible past, the speaker tortures himself as he once again considers the despicable actions that led to his murder of his wife. For some strange reason, he found himself attracted more toward animals than humans:

> There is something in the unselfish and self-sacrificing love of a brute, which goes directly to the heart of him who has had frequent occasion to test the paltry friendship and gossamer fidelity of mere *Man*. (850)

At this point the reader knows that such an unusual outlook will cause nothing but trouble for this disturbed man. He has buried himself in a form of misanthropy that makes him value animals over his fellow men. One creature in particular intrigues him--a huge black cat. Reading the speaker's description of the cat and following the events in the tale, the members of Poe's audience would no doubt agree with the numerous modern critics who view this feline as an incarnate demon.[39] When the narrator's superstitious wife raises the possibility of the cat's being a witch in disguise she echoes traditional demon lore. Many individuals still believe that animals serve as familiars. When the protagonist downplays this point, we must suspect that he is guilty of making an understatement that overstates.

The name of this old cat--Pluto--conjures images of the death awaiting the narrator at the conclusion. The animal constantly follows him, just as death relentlessly pursues all humans. Gradually the speaker's temperament changes and he grows increasingly hostile. Although he attributes this transformation to excessive drink, we suspect that the demon-cat has something to do with it as well. In a drunken stupor the man mutilates the beast by gouging one of its eyes with a knife. This impromptu surgery may represent the speaker's attempt to remove the all-powerful eye of a devil who was exerting an unholy influence over him. The demon's orb, however, has penetrated the narrator's psychic defenses and corroded his moral faculty. As the tale proceeds toward its conclusion the man's corruption markedly increases.

Poe's speaker (whose philosophy resembles that of the condemned narrator in "The Imp of the Perverse") makes a curious statement concerning the human propensity toward repulsive actions:

> Yet I am not more sure that my soul lives, than I am that perverseness is one of the primitive impulses of the human heart--one of the indivisible primary faculties, or sentiments, which give direction to the character of Man. Who has not, a hundred times, found himself committing a vile or a silly action, for no other reason than because he knows he should *not*? (852)

On the surface the narrator seems to be justifying his hanging of the cat. More important, these remarks illustrate Poe's theory regarding man and many of his desires. Evil frightens *and* captivates. Many people find the wish to perform a horrible act strangely attractive. Horror, perversion, and disgust entice mankind. At one time or another each human being dreams of performing some incredibly violent sin. Aware of this fact, Poe uses horror and fear to lure his characters and readers into the hellish land of terror and depravity. He understands fully the leanings of humanity.

Immediately following the cat's death terrible events befall the narrator. Such occurrences make the reader wonder if the tale should be subtitled "The Demon's Revenge." On the night of the day the feline is exterminated a terrible conflagration engulfs the man's home. Cruel flames suggest hell fire. Losing his entire life savings, the speaker visits the rubble and discovers a truly horrible manifestation of his tormentor: "I approached and saw, as if graven in *bas relief* upon the white surface, the figure of gigantic *cat. . . .* There was a rope about the animal's neck" (853). The narrator seems to view some sort of huge idol, and the charred ruins become a type of demonic temple. Fear swells in his bosom as he tries to explain rationally this strange apparition. He comforts himself, but only temporarily.

The protagonist soon decides that he needs another animal companion. He finds a cat that closely resembles Pluto and cares for him. Here we immediately suspect that this creature is the reincarnation of the demon-cat. Poe employs a variation of the transmigration-of-souls motif that he used so successfully in earlier tales. This animal, missing an eye, arouses hatred and fear in the man: "With my aversion to this cat, however, its partiality for myself seemed to increase" (855). The demon is no doubt pleased by the man's increasing moral decay. Describing his own fear, the narrator remarks that his misgivings were "not exactly a dread of physical evil . . ." (855). He seems suspicious of the cat and must feel that the creature might possibly be a demon luring him to damnation. Once the white patch on the animal's breast assumes the shape of a gallows, the protagonist receives a vision of the fate in store for him.

Influenced by the horrible animal, the narrator reveals how "evil thoughts became my sole intimates--the darkest and most evil of thoughts" (856). He eventually kills his wife and, antici- pating the brick work of Montresor, walls up the corpse in his cellar. When the police come to investigate his wife's disappear- ance, he exhibits a bravado not unlike that of the narrator in

"The Tell-Tale Heart." As his perversity has increased so too has his self-esteem.[40] He taps on the masonry behind which lies the body of his wife and hears a terrifying sound: "a wailing shriek, half of horror and half of triumph, such as might have arisen only out of hell, conjointly from the throats of the damned in their agony and of the demons that exult in the damnation" (859). This odd noise could conceivably be a combination of the screams made by both the demon-cat, the victorious devil who prepares to welcome another soul into the brotherhood of Satan, *and* the narrator himself, who, suddenly realizing that he is doomed by his horrible action and that he has been conquered by the strange cat, shouts in terror. The third voice contributing to the tumult of the scene belongs to the reader, who reacts to the fears that Poe scatters throughout this tale of cosmic dread.

"THE PREMATURE BURIAL," "THE SYSTEM OF DOCTOR TARR AND PROFESSOR FETHER," "THE FACTS IN THE CASE OF M. VALDEMAR," "THE CASK OF AMONTILLADO," AND "HOP-FROG"

The double-edged sword of "The Premature Burial" allows Poe to exploit two areas that his readers found particularly alluring. Scholars note that tales dealing with hastily performed interments were extremely popular during the mid-nineteenth century.[41] Poe's story, therefore, reflects his awareness of current literary trends. Knowledgeable in the field of psychology, he also realizes that the mental terrors arising from the consideration of such a state fascinate his audience. This tale, then, seeks to arouse and take advantage of one of the most horrifying fears present in the mind.

The tale opens with what seems to be Poe's attempt to vindicate horror fiction from the charge of excessive morbidity. He writes that stories that portray actual historical events, no matter how horrible, are accepted by the public, whereas tales of *fictional* horror are labelled abhorrent. Reality triumphs over imagination in such cases. Mocking these notions, Poe disguises his piece as one of the numerous medical articles that were frequently published in popular journals of the period. Fully cognizant that his readers thrill "with the most intense of 'pleasurable pain'" (955) whenever they peruse a work dealing with extreme human calamity, he creates a tale that bears the mark of an expert writer well-versed in the intricacies of Gothic fiction.

Almost immediately Poe sets out to isolate each of his readers and entangle his audience in a web of fear: "true wretchedness . . . ultimate wo[e]--is particular, not diffuse" (955). Although dread is a universal emotion, Poe heightens its effect by informing each member of his audience that he must grapple with this anxiety all alone. Next the narrator states directly the ultimate terror that the sons of Adam may one day be forced to endure:

> To be buried alive, is, beyond question, the most terrific of these extremes which has ever fallen to the lot of mere mortality. That it has frequently, very frequently, so fallen, will scarcely be denied by those who think. (955)

In the manner of his fellow magazinists, Poe substantiates this statement by producing actual case histories of people who had been buried alive. These examples contain passages that echo those appearing in some of Poe's earlier fear sketches. For instance, he tells us of the wife of a prominent Baltimore citizen who was overpowered by an "unaccountable illness, which completely baffled the skill of her physicians" (956). This sentence is almost identical with that describing Madeline Usher. The case of the Parisian love triangle features a young suitor who, believing his beloved dead, rushes to the cemetery "with the romantic purpose of disinterring the corpse, and possessing himself of its luxuriant tresses" (957). Here the reader is reminded of a similar man--Egaeus--and his desire to remove Berenice's teeth. By calling his audience's attention to some of his previous tales of dread, Poe hopes to increase the impact of fear in this work.

Poe strives relentlessly to frighten readers. Discussing a peasant who feels someone struggling beneath him in an attempt to free himself from a grave, the narrator states that at first no person believed the man: "But his evident terror, and the dogged obstinacy with which he persisted in his story, had at length their natural effect upon the crowd" (958-959). Poe seems to warn his audience that, like the peasant, he will persist in relating such horrors until they feel the "natural effect" of intense dread. Concluding this section of "tangible proofs," Poe relates the case of Mr. Stapleton. Buried alive, Stapleton's body is exhumed by grave robbers employed by a local medical school. Such ghoulish criminals frequented graveyards during the period and wrought terror in the hearts and minds of many nineteenth-century citizens. Seeking to increase further a reader's anxieties regarding premature burial, the narrator (manipulated carefully by Poe) remarks chillingly: "When we reflect how very rarely, from the nature of the case, we have it in our power to detect them, we must admit that they may *frequently* occur without our cognizance" (961). Each reader is warned that he could become the next victim.

Our narrator now directs his attention toward his own encounter with this form of enclosure. This unfortunate soul lives in constant fear of such a fate. Burial before death produces acute bodily and mental distress, and the speaker painstakingly itemizes the sensations that befall the prematurely entombed individual:

> The unendurable oppression of the lungs--the stifling
> fumes of the damp earth--the clinging of the death
> garments--the rigid embrace of the narrow house--the
> blackness of the absolute Night--the silence like a sea
> that overwhelms--the unseen but palpable presence of
> the Conqueror Worm--these things . . . carry into the
> heart, which still palpitates, a degree of appalling and
> intolerable horror from which the most daring imagina-
> tion must recoil. (961)

Similar feelings no doubt swell in the bosom of the reader in
glancing at this terrifying passage and reacting to death's
darkness and decay. Continuing his story, the protagonist reveals
that fear of premature burial overcame him to the point where
all of his thoughts were directed toward this phenomenon. He
has a disturbing dream in which the figure of Death presents
him with a truly horrifying scene. This sinister figure opens all
the graves of mankind and uncovers a startling fact: "But, alas!
the real sleepers were fewer, by many millions, than those who
slumbered not at all" (964). Even Death feels pity for the many
unfortunate individuals who were buried alive. Dread constantly
harasses the narrator. He states that "my nerves became
thoroughly unstrung, and I fell a prey to perpetual horror"
(965). Eventually he is victimized by his own extreme fear.
Travelling on the James River in a small sloop, he lies down in
a tiny berth that suggests the confines of the grave. He imagines
that he has become a living tenant of the tomb but is soon
awakened by the crew. Although he had experienced a vision
engendered by psychic misgivings, he readily admits that "the
tortures endured, however, were undoubtedly quite equal, for
the time, to those of actual sepulture. They were fearfully--they
were inconceivably hideous" (968). The protagonist's words
attest fear's supreme power.

Poe's two concluding paragraphs might puzzle readers. Here
the writer seems to downplay fear fiction and reject its unique
strengths. Careful examination, however, shows that Poe

employs psychological tricks in these passages. The speaker comments that his cataleptic condition vanishes once he discards his charnel apprehensions: "I thought upon other subjects than Death. . . . I read no . . . fustian about church-yards--no bugaboo tales--*such as this*" (969). Is Poe discrediting his own fiction? Perhaps in reality he is issuing a warning to feeble hearts, fully aware that readers will not heed it. The perversities lodged in the human mind dictate that people quite frequently do what they are told not to do. When Poe writes "Alas! the grim legion of sepulchral terrors cannot be regarded as altogether fanciful--but . . . they must sleep, or they will devour us--they must be suffered to slumber, or we perish" (969), he does so out of a knowledge of the mind's curious attraction toward dread and pain. On the literal level, Poe does not want to see people succumb to actual death. As a writer of Gothic tales, however, he does wish that his readers experience a vicarious destruction through the act of reading terror literature. His words, therefore, admonish *and* entice.

On the surface, Poe's "The System of Doctor Tarr and Professor Fether" seems to satirize the lenient, humane treatment of mental patients. Numerous critics view this study of insanity as one in which parodic elements play a central part.[42] Although these opinions contribute greatly to our understanding and appreciation of this tale, they might prevent the reader from encountering the troubling message lurking beneath the satiric surface. Indeed, "Tarr and Fether" discusses one of the nineteenth-century citizen's most vulnerable phobic pressure points-- the fear of slave rebellions.

Pro-slavery thought was rampant during the period. Following slave-led insurrections such as those of Haiti in 1800, Denmark Vesey in 1822, and Nat Turner in 1831, the dread of similar uprisings markedly increased in the minds of white slaveholders.[43] We must recall that Poe considered himself a Southerner. He openly embraced the South's way of life and its unique philosophical standpoints. Whereas certain scholars persist in debating the fact, one can conclude that Poe readily accepted the opinion stating that slavery was morally justifiable and economically necessary and also dreaded the possibility of future slave revolts.[44] The "Paulding-Drayton Review," a work that many students of American literature believe came from the pen of Poe, states clearly its author's thoughts regarding Blacks.[45] "Tarr and Fether" reflects Poe's concern for one of the most volatile issues of his day. Relying on both social and psychological misgivings, he contemplates what to the nineteenth-century reader was a most disturbing possibility.

The tale opens in the autumn of the year, the season of decay and the falling off of vitality in nature. As the narrator tours "the extreme Southern provinces of France" (1002), he prepares to visit a madhouse. This *Maison de Santé* employs the renowned "soothing system," which advocates the gentle treatment of inmates. Since he approaches the building on horseback, we recall immediately the unpleasant experiences that awaited two of Poe's other equestrian-protagonists, Metzengerstein and Roderick Usher's companion. Like these unfortunate horsemen, the narrator in this tale will encounter bewildering and hostile forces bent on the destruction of the established order once he meets the madmen who have subdued their guards and assumed control of the asylum. Here we should note that in line with the story's purpose, the mental hospital represents a Southern plantation while the patients symbolize rebellious slaves who attempt to destroy their masters.

Images of darkness and enclosure soon accost speaker and reader. Nearing the sanitarium, the narrator and his acquaintance "entered a grass-grown by-path, which, in half an hour, nearly lost itself in a dense forest, clothing the base of a mountain. Through this dank and gloomy wood we rode some two miles" (1003). Surrounded by blackness, the protagonist receives a foreshadowing of the sinister adventure that will befall him once he enters the hospital. The building itself adds to the speaker's fears: "It was a fantastic *château*, much dilapidated, and indeed scarcely tenantable through age and neglect.

Its aspect inspired me with absolute dread . . ." (1003). He reacts in much the same fashion as the narrator in "Usher" does when he first observes Roderick's home. Southerners of the times pondering the reality of slave insurrections would probably respond similarly.

Entering the asylum and meeting its proprietor, Monsieur Maillard, the protagonist reveals his interest in the famous "soothing system" that has apparently revolutionized the treatment of the insane:

> the institution . . . was managed upon what is vulgarly termed the "system of soothing"--that all punishments were avoided--that even confinement was seldom resorted to--that the patients, while secretly watched, were left much apparent liberty, and that most of them were permitted to roam about the house and grounds. . . . (1004)

Poe seems to describe one of the many theories intended to improve the conditions under which slaves were forced to exist. As the tale progresses we see that he derides such humanitarian feelings by showing the unpleasant circumstances to which they give birth. The people of Paris, undoubtedly meant to represent the Northern reformers and abolitionists who sought to influence their Southern brethren, fail to realize the danger inherent in the attempt to alter the *status quo*. Maillard, himself one of the rebels, states that he abandoned the soothing system because the prisoners "were often aroused to a dangerous frenzy by injudicious persons who called to inspect the house" (1005). Once again Poe takes a poke at the many "moralists" who wanted to modify the institution of slavery. Further remarks suggest the opinions held by Northerners concerning the South's radical theories. The speaker comments that "I remembered having been informed, in Paris, that the southern provincialists were a peculiarly eccentric people, with a vast number of antiquated notions . . ." (1008). An apparent adherent to the Northern view, he will discover the chaos resulting from slave upheavals.

Commenting on the inmates' proclivities, the speaker explains such occurrences in terms often used to describe characteristics associated with the Black slaves in the nineteenth century. The patients' fondness for amusements such as music, dance, and various other trivial pursuits conjures images of slaves relaxing after a hard day's work. Here Poe codedly cautions his fellows not to be disarmed by such revelry, as the Black possesses a savage cunning and is fully capable of violent displays of emotion. Later when the deposed guards wail in the hope of attracting attention, the narrator comments on the reaction of the "inmates": "They all grew as pale as so many corpses, and, shrinking within their seats, sat quivering and gibbering with terror . . ." (1014). Traditional beliefs hold that slaves were easily "spooked" by strange, unexpected noises. The words of Maillard further suggest one of the nineteenth-century slave's favorite entertainments *and* the white man's reaction to these attempts at amusement: "The lunatics, every now and then, get up a howl in concert; one starting another, as is sometimes the case with a bevy of dogs at night" (1015). Here Poe comments on the Black's propensity toward song. Earlier in the story the narrator remarked that the music produced by the madmen proved extremely offensive. One gets the impression that these creatures are animals who are miraculously capable of walking upright. The number of patients who fancy themselves frogs, donkeys, or chickens reinforces this notion.

Despite the apparent harmlessness of these creatures, Poe warns that these mentally inferior beings must not be trusted: "His cunning . . . is proverbial, and great. If he has a project in view, he conceals his design with a marvelous wisdom. . . . When a madman appears *thoroughly* sane, indeed, it is high time to put him in a straight jacket" (1018). Poe suggests that when the slave appears particularly subservient he is often most dangerous. Reflecting a typically conservative Southern viewpoint, he hints that small doses of freedom will infect the slave with the fever of wanton destruction. Maillard echoes this sentiment when he remarks on the effects of the soothing system on the lunatics:

> They behaved remarkably well--especially so--any one of sense might have known that some devilish scheme was brewing from that particular fact, that the fellows behaved so *remarkably* well. And, sure enough, one fine morning the keepers found themselves pinioned hand and foot, and thrown into . . . cells. (1018)

Once he observes the escaped guards, who ironically resemble the chimpanzees and orangutans of Africa, the narrator learns that the benefits of a harsher treatment of inmates seem to outweigh those of a more lenient system. In "Tarr and Fether," then, Poe advises his fellow Southerners to beware of their slaves. Aware of the terrifying aspects of blackness,[46] Poe uses this social and mental fear to appeal to the darker leanings of his audience.

As he had done in "Silence" and "Masque," Poe relies on the fear of death in "The Facts in the Case of M. Valdemar" to horrify his reader. Similar to "The Premature Burial," this sketch is presented as a "factual" account of the studies conducted by a renowned mesmerist. As is evident in many of his other works, Poe relies on the appeal inherent in one of the period's most popular topics. He does not restrict his interest to the wonders of hypnotic prowess, however. Taking full advantage of the human dread of death and the decay that accompanies it, he creates a tale that emphasizes the repulsive physical changes wrought by the great shadow, death. "Valdemar," then, shocks its audience with gory images of fetid decomposition. This piece resembles "Berenice" in that it assumes many of the characteristics of a typical literary potboiler. If we recall Philip Pendleton Cooke's reaction upon reading the story, we comprehend the intensity of this masterpiece of fear fiction. The dread of the loss of physical identity after death and of the terror of bodily transformation makes certain that Poe will succeed in his attempt to subdue psychically his shuddering following.

In the opening of the tale the narrator implies the ominous nature of his experiment by expressing the wish "of all parties concerned, to keep the affair from the public . . ." (1233). We might recall the desire of Mary Shelley's Dr. Frankenstein to shroud his scientific activities in secrecy. Those who seek to explore and expose the secrets of life and death tread on delicate ground. Whatever information they might unearth could conceivably lead to trouble. Perhaps our speaker suffers from the same curiosity that affected Mary Shelley's inquisitive doctor. Such suspicions prove feasible once we learn that the hypnotist seeks to discover the true power of his art and observe "to what extent, or for how long a period, the encroachments of Death might be arrested . . ." (1233). Poe's protagonist states that the consequences of this test might prove to be of immense importance. Like Victor Frankenstein, he wants to preserve life indefinitely. Whereas this idea appeals to many individuals, Poe eventually shows that such human efforts to arrest the oncoming of Death prove futile.

Visiting the dying man on whom he will perform his mesmeric experiment, the narrator describes the gentleman's deplorable physical condition:

> I had not seen him for ten days, and was appalled by the fearful alteration which the brief interval had wrought in him. His face wore a leaden hue; the eyes were utterly lustreless; and the emaciation was so extreme that the skin had been broken through by the cheek-bones. His expectoration was excessive. (1235)

The approach of death brings with it the disgusting transformation that overpowers its victim. In this scene Poe takes full advantage of the uneasiness arising from the thought of corporeal decay. Later he will heighten the effect of this idea with an episode of almost unbearable revulsion.

Valdemar sinks deeper into the realms of darkness and the speaker determines that he must now mesmerize the sufferer. Gazing directly into the dying man's eyes, the narrator seems to be beckoning the soul of this afflicted individual. In a sense he hopes that his glance will be capable of exerting a strong influence on the spiritual essence residing in Valdemar. Poe now employs a variation of the evil-eye motif that he used in such sketches as "The Tell-Tale Heart" and "The Black Cat." Acting in a fashion not unlike a demon's, the mesmerist attempts to gain control of the ultimate life force. As we shall see, his triumph is merely temporary.

Under the mesmerist's influence, Valdemar appears soothed by the preserving power of the spell. Yet his bodily position portends gloom: "The legs were at full length; the arms were nearly so, and reposed on the bed at a moderate distance from the loins. The head was very slightly elevated" (1237). The slumberer reclines as if he has been deposited in a coffin. These events occur at midnight, and the witching hour intensifies the aura of blackness that engulfs the chamber. Up to this point the speaker is satisfied with the results of this trial. Commenting on Valdemar's condition, he remarks that "the general appearance was certainly not that of death" (1238). He questions Valdemar and finds that the act of dying bears a strong likeness to a form of peaceful sleep. This placid scene is soon shattered by the death agonies that accompany the arrival of Valdemar's, and by implication, of man's end. Poe again relies on the disgust arising from humanity's perception of a body yielding to the corrosive embrace of nature: "I presume that no member of the party then present had been unaccustomed to death-bed horrors; but so hideous beyond conception was the appearance of M. Valdemar at this moment, that there was a general shrinking back from the region of the bed" (1239). A voice now emerges from the "corpse," and the mesmerist has apparently succeeded.

The sound, however, unnerves its listeners as it seems to come from a great distance. It possesses a "gelatinous or glutinous" quality that troubles the scientist. When the preserved body informs its audience that it is indeed dead, many of the people present faint or flee in terror. The deceased remains in this condition for seven months. Once again Poe uses this ill-omened number to suggest some sort of impending horror.

The concluding scene attests death's ultimate victory. Breaking the trance, the protagonist notices that as he passes his hand over Valdemar a pungent and offensive yellow discharge flows from beneath the corpse's eyelids. Suddenly a voice issues from the body: "'For God's sake!--quick!--quick!--put me to sleep--or, quick!--waken me!--quick!--*I say to you that I am dead!*'" (1242). The urgency with which these words are uttered implies that Valdemar is ready to meet the spectre of death. Perhaps his seven months of suspended animation have been uncomfortable in the sense that they have prevented him from experiencing the blissful repose of eternity toward which all creation moves. Upset, the narrator arouses the sleep-waker and observes the absolutely disgusting result:

> his whole frame at once--within the space of a single minute, or even less, shrunk--crumbled--absolutely *rotted* away beneath my hands. Upon the bed, before that whole company, there lay a nearly liquid mass of loathsome--of detestable putridity. (1243)

Having lost what remained of his physical identity, Valdemar now assumes the spiritual qualities of a citizen of the afterlife. Heretofore he was held prisoner by the mesmeric abilities of the narrator. Human vanity makes man dread the decay of his corporeal essence. But the preservation of Valdemar's body seems to trouble him to the point where he eagerly awaits the conqueror worm. As disgusting as physical decomposition is, it reflects the workings of a natural process. Man should not interfere with nature's design. "The Facts in the Case of M.

Valdemar," then, uses fear of death to terrify and enlighten its readers.

The overall effect in "The Cask of Amontillado," another in this group of tales, depends a great deal on the dread of premature burial, enclosure, darkness, and death. Besides counting on the disturbing results arising from these reservations, Poe also presents a classic tale of revenge reminiscent of the popular plays produced in Elizabethan England.[47] Set in Italy, "Cask" reveals the blueprint of Montresor's plan for the destruction of his hated foe Fortunato. We see that the speaker will slowly and cruelly subdue his prey. Bordering on madness, the mind of Montresor permits Poe to explore once more the dark abyss of human depravity. As he journeys through this dangerous land he intends to thrill and horrify.

The opening sentence brings Montresor's intentions to light. A sense of dark, hellish vengeance envelops the scene as he reveals that "I must not only punish, but punish with impunity" (1256). The narrator's demonic qualities become even more evident when he discusses what he considers to be his fool-proof plan:

> It must be understood that neither by word nor deed had I given Fortunato cause to doubt my good will. I continued, as was my wont, to smile in his face, and he did not perceive that my smile *now* was at the thought of his immolation. (1257)

Aware of his enemy's weak point, Montresor will use Fortunato's love of wine to effect his dissolution. Hubris will play a part in destroying this self-proclaimed connoisseur. Biding his time, the speaker awaits the proper moment to set his scheme in motion.

Italy's carnival season provides a fitting and ironic background for the implementation of Montresor's revenge. Poe states that the darkness of evening is about to enshroud the festivities. The blackness parallels that of Montresor's unholy design and foreshadows that which Fortunato will experience once he is walled in his crypt. We learn that a sense of supreme madness permeates this chaotic scene. Such revelry suggests the disordered mental states of both Montresor and Fortunato. The schemer has become mad with the idea of vengeance. All of his efforts have been directed toward achieving his overpowering, sinister aim. His victim, on the other hand, is overcome by the irrationality resulting from excessive drink. Poe also implies that Fortunato seems prone to perform foolish actions. Dressed in the colorful costume of a clown he becomes a most ludicrous figure indeed. His ultimate peccancy, however, must have been his offending Montresor and arousing his feelings of hatred. Upon meeting his quarry, Montresor remarks "I was so pleased to see him that I thought I should never have done wringing his hand" (1257). The irony here is crystal clear: the protagonist would much more prefer to wring Fortunato's neck.

Convincing his drunken companion to accompany him to the family wine-cellar, Montresor takes Fortunato to his aptly named "vaults." All the while he implores his associate to return to the festival, knowing full well that such words will only increase Fortunato's desire to visit what will soon become his mausoleum. Before leaving for his home Montresor dons a black silk mask and a cloak.[48] By covering his face he becomes a figure remotely similar to the mysterious guest present in "Masque." Both of these beings carry death with them. Perhaps Montresor employs such a disguise in order to conceal any evil intentions present in his face from the many revellers that he must no doubt pass on the way to his palazzo. Clad in such a fashion, he resembles a dark shadow that longs to possess the soul of its intended victim.

When the two men approach their destination, Poe clearly shows that the depths of the home serve more as catacombs than as a conventional wine-cellar. Descending into the cavernous charnel house, Montresor and Fortunato seem to plummet into the abyss of hell itself. The decay evident in these passageways suggests the decomposition that awaits all occupants of the grave. Walls encrusted with nitre imply that Montresor's revenge will soon explode and annihilate his rival. Fortunato suffers from coughing fits that grow more severe as he proceeds downwards into the core of this damp tomb. Feigning an interest in his friend's health, the narrator utters "'your health is precious. You are rich, respected, admired, beloved; you are happy, as once I was'" (1259). Later he states that his family was once a great and famous race. Here we receive the impression that Fortunato has in some manner brought about the Montresors' downfall. The Montresor family crest supports this notion: "'A huge human foot d'or, in a field azure; the foot crushes a serpent rampant whose fangs are imbedded in the heel'" (1259). This coat of arms presents a scene of mutual destruction. Crushing the serpent, the huge foot is subjected to the snake's poisonous bite. As Montresor was defeated by Fortunato, so too will the drunken nobleman feel the wrath of his deranged host.

Travelling far beneath the river's bed, the comrades enter a world of death and darkness:

> We passed through a range of low arches, descended, passed on, and descending again, arrived at a deep crypt, in which the foulness of the air caused our flambeaux rather to glow than flame. . . . Its walls had been lined with human remains, piled to the vault overhead. . . . (1260-1261)

Gradually they proceed toward the niche that will serve as Fortunato's tomb. This area seems to heighten the feeling of enclosure that these gloomy surroundings produce: "we perceived a *still* [my italics] interior recess, in depth about four feet, in width three, in height six or seven" (1261). This silent room seems cursed with the quiet Poe often associates with death. It also appears as a sort of vertical grave. Montresor soon manages to chain up Fortunato inside this depression. Poe now uses the dread produced by the prospect of premature interment when he has Montresor slowly wall in his prey within this dark enclosure. As his intoxication wears off, Fortunato realizes his predicament and screams in terror. This noise frightens the speaker, but he soon regains his composure and replies to these shrieks with shouts of his own. Sweet posits that Montresor reacts in this fashion because he unconsciously sees part of himself in Fortunato.[49] In all likelihood such behavior results from the fact that Montresor, mad with revenge, momentarily loses his equanimity and mocks his helpless victim. Eventually no sound emerges from the crypt and the narrator seems upset by the death-like silence. Perhaps he is disappointed by the thought that his prisoner has died too quickly and avoided the slow, horrible fate planned for him.[50] A master of artistic effect, Poe in "Cask" does not disappoint the audience that seeks to journey into the domain of fear. This tale, in a sense, entombs its readers in their own cellars of mental dread.

One of Poe's last tales, "Hop-Frog" focuses on the concept of revenge in much the same manner of "Cask," although important distinctions are evident. The reader never learns exactly what Fortunato did to incur Montresor's wrath. This tale remains one of remarkable subtlety. "Hop-Frog," on the other hand, illustrates clearly how the fat, jovial king aroused the hellish emotions of his dwarf. Besides incorporating traditional psychic fears into this sketch, Poe also returns to a subject he treated at length in "Tarr and Fether"--the danger of slave insurrections.[51] This widespread phobic pressure point permits Poe to produce one of his most captivating and upsetting stories of Gothic horror.

Early in the tale we learn that the boisterous monarch loves practical jokes. His seven ministers share his outlook. The attentive reader notes immediately the presence of that "magic" number seven again. The king and his associates will meet an end similar to the unpleasant experiences that befall the seven companions in "Shadow" and the people who occupy the seven rooms in "Masque." Sinister omens are present in the opening passages. Poe increases his audience's misgivings when he introduces the tale's central character, the crippled dwarf Hop-

Frog. Familiar with the conventions of folk literature, the nineteenth-century reader would view such a creature with a fearful, suspicious eye. Most dwarves in fiction possess devilish traits that link them to the nether regions. We shall see that Poe's jester is no exception.

Various passages suggest that Poe uses this tale to comment on the master-slave relationship. In order to increase the terror in his reader's mind, Poe seems to combine the dwarf of tradition with the Black slave of reality. This literary commingling strikes deeply at the subconscious dread residing in the nineteenth-century American audience. The description of Hop-Frog stresses the animal qualities of this seemingly harmless individual:

> the prodigious muscular power which nature seemed to
> have bestowed upon his arms . . . enabled him to
> perform many feats of wonderful dexterity, where trees
> or ropes were in question, or anything else to climb. At
> such exercises he certainly much more resembled a . . .
> small monkey, than a frog. (1346)

Masters would often describe their slaves as if these servants were actually some form of simian. In addition, nineteenth-century racial theorists thought of Blacks as incredibly strong and agile animals. Hop-Frog's native country appears reminiscent of the darker regions of Africa, and it seems that he was removed from his land of origin by a marauding band of slave-traders: "It was from some barbarous region . . . that no person ever heard of--a vast distance from the court of our king. Hop-Frog, and a young girl . . . had been forcibly carried off from their respective homes in adjoining provinces, and sent as presents to the king . . ." (1346). Both Hop-Frog and Tripetta provide the court with much levity. They amuse their masters with dance, song, and jest. These entertainers, in turn, are considered nothing more than harmless, talented pets. Slaveholders viewed their servants in a similar light and would often treat them in a cruel manner identical to that which the tale's two dwarves must endure.

Once the king decides to present a masquerade we recall the celebration of Prince Prospero and the costume party atmosphere of "Cask." This portly ruler and his corpulent cabinet members will eventually be undone at this carefree gathering. Finding the dwarf's vulnerability to alcohol hilarious, the king makes him drink. The jester tearfully accepts the wine and "many large, bitter drops fell into the goblet as he took it, humbly, from the hand of the tyrant" (1348). Here we recall the drops with which Ligeia destroyed the Lady Rowena. In "Hop-Frog," however, Poe gives this episode a slight twist. Rowena was killed by a poison administered by a hostile, external force. Hop-Frog becomes influenced by the rage that swells within him. The galling taste of the tear-salted wine helps to bring the dwarf's sour thoughts to the surface.

When the king treats Tripetta cruelly, Hop-Frog decides that he must now rebel against this despotic sovereign. A dead silence afflicts the scene and this stillness foreshadows what awaits the heartless masters. Such death-like quiet is shattered by a horrible grating sound that fills the room and brings dread to the listeners. Infuriated, the ruler asks the jester if he had been making the noise: "Hereupon the dwarf laughed . . . and displayed a set of large, powerful, and very repulsive teeth" (1349). Poe again stresses the cripple's animal characteristics. Unaware of the very real danger presented by this creature, the king and his ministers agree with the dwarf when he offers to dress them as orangutans for their costume ball. These foolish frolickers seem incapable of suspecting their slave of any chicanery. How could such an amusing being arouse any misgivings? Whereas these royal masqueraders leave themselves vulnerable, the reader is fully aware of Hop-Frog's evil intent.

Poe apparently expresses what he considers to be the typical slave's opinion regarding his master when he has his dwarf describe the realistic costumes he is preparing for his victims: "'The resemblance shall be so striking, that the company . . . will take you for *real beasts* [my italics] --and of course, they will be as much terrified as astonished'" (1350). Sublime aspects will be evident even in this horrible situation. Reacting to the scene, the guests will experience dread *and* wonder. Once he coats his prey with tar, Hop-Frog continues to implement his demonic design. Now black and chained, the king and his advisers become the slaves of the dwarf and undergo an ironic role reversal. Unknown to them, they have now become the cripple's chattels. These bizarre creatures will soon learn that their laughter was indeed unwise.

The time arrives for Hop-Frog to execute his well-wrought scheme of revenge. Poe states that the room in which the masquerade was to take place was circular and dark. Both the shape of this chamber and its lack of natural light suggest the endlessness of eternity and the blackness of death. At the symbolic hour of midnight, the victims make their appearance. Hop-Frog has chained the men together in order to increase verisimilitude. In reality, this binding will allow him to destroy all of his tormentors at once. We learn that the many people in the crowd felt uncomfortable because of the close quarters in which they were placed. Fear of enclosure plays a role here, and Poe's revelation that Hop-Frog has locked the doors intensifies this uneasiness. Clinging to the chain that dangles from the roof, Hop-Frog and the "apes" are hoisted toward the skylight. Again we see that a dead silence ensues, only to be broken by the harsh, grating sound that "came from the fang-like teeth of the dwarf, who ground them and gnashed them as he foamed at the mouth, and glared, with an expression of maniacal rage, into the upturned countenances of the king and his seven companions" (1353). Now the demon qualities of this rebellious slave become undeniably evident. He ignites the tar and flax and incinerates the tyrant and his compatriots. As the other guests watched helplessly, "The eight corpses swung in their chains, a fetid, blackened, hideous, and indistinguishable mass" (1354).

Readers who view this tale as a treatise on the issue of slavery might conclude that Poe advocates the humane treatment of bondsmen. Such scholars must recall the remarks made in "Tarr and Fether." There and in "Hop-Frog" the author implicitly warns his fellow Southerners not to underestimate the slave's ability to rebel. Far from being a docile, domesticated pet, the Black must be considered a dangerous, wild animal capable of demonic violence. This social dread and the psychological fears evident in "Hop-Frog" demonstrate how Poe takes advantage of his audience's psychic soft spots.

NOTES

1. Thompson, *Poe's Fiction*, pp. 52-65.
2. Benjamin Franklin Fisher IV, "Poe's 'Metzengerstein': Not a Hoax," *American Literature* 42 (January 1971): 488. See Fisher's later observations in *The Very Spirit of Cordiality: The Literary Uses of Alcohol and Alcoholism in the Tales of Edgar Allan Poe* (Baltimore: The Edgar Allan Poe Society, 1978), p. 3; and David H. Hirsch, "Poe's 'Metzengerstein' as a Tale of the Subconscious," *University of Mississippi Studies in English*, n.s. 3 (1982): 40-52. The most recent opinion, that of Kenneth Silverman in *Edgar A. Poe: Mournful and Never-ending Remembrance* (New York: Harper Collins, 1991), pp. 88-90, 467, note, argues against a comic reading as put forth by Thompson. Silverman finds the tale recognizably in the (serious) Gothic vein of the times.
3. The "evil eye" (bewitching by means of a glance) appears in much of the world's folklore. One popular variation states that a person with the power of the evil eye cannot look at any living thing before breaking fast in the morning without causing it to wither and die. An old Irish legend speaks of an evil god possessing an evil eye, while another version links this ocular phenomenon with the one-eyed anti-Christ. See Stith Thompson, *Motif-Index of Folk-Literature* (Bloomington, Ind.: Indiana University Press, 1955-1958), 1: 80, 192; 2: 364-366.
4. For the various Irish, Lithuanian, and German folklores linking horses to the devil see Stith Thompson, 3: 326, 333, 340; 4: 494. According to one German version, the devil can disappear in a carriage driven by four black horses. Perhaps Poe viewed a variation of this motif appropriate when he has the "devilish" Metzengerstein carried off by his hellish steed. An old Irish legend states that horses were frequently sent into an enemy's camp to cause stampedes. The horse in "Metzengerstein" certainly causes a commotion when it

suddenly appears in the Baron's stables and, to a degree, "stampedes" Metzengerstein into hell.

5. Tzvetan Todorov, *The Fantastic: A Structural Approach to a Literary Genre*, trans. Richard Howard (Cleveland: The Press of Case Western Reserve University, 1973), p. 33.

6. The mysterious ship described by Poe suggests the legendary Flying Dutchman. Stith Thompson notes that the origin of this motif rests in two stories. One variation states that a sea captain's cruelty is punished by his having to sail his phantom ship eternally with no hope of finding a safe harbor, while another version states that the ship must sail forever because its captain defied a storm. See 4: 472.

7. For comments on Poe's revisions of "MS. Found" (along with a reprint of the original Baltimore *Saturday Visiter* version), see Fisher's *The Very Spirit of Cordiality*, pp. 5-7, 19-32.

8. Nina Baym, "The Function of Poe's Pictorialism," *South Atlantic Quarterly* 65 (Winter 1966): 50.

9. Consult David Ketterer, "The Sexual Abyss: Consummation in 'The Assignation,'" *Poe Studies* 19 (1986): 7-10, for an interesting reading of this tale. For different viewpoints from Ketterer's, see Fisher's readings in *The Library Chronicle* 39 (Spring 1973): 89-105, and *The Library Chronicle* 40 (Winter 1976): 221-251, as well as his "The Flights of a Good Man's Mind: Gothic Fantasy in Poe's 'The Assignation,'" *Modern Language Studies* 16 (Summer 1986): 27-34; Dennis Pahl, "Recovering Byron: Poe's 'The Assignation,'" *Criticism* 26 (Spring 1984): 111-119, which reappears as Chapter 2 of his book *Architects of the Abyss: The Indeterminate Fictions of Poe, Hawthorne, and Melville* (Columbia: University of Missouri Press, 1989); and George H. Soule, "Byronism in Poe's 'Metzengerstein' and 'William Wilson,'" *ESQ: A Journal of the American Renaissance* 24 (Third Quarter 1978): 152-162.

10. The presence of seven comrades in this story suggests the mysterious significance of the number "7." This mystical

number plays an important role in world folklore and, depending on the culture, has both good and evil connotations. Many religions use the number as a sign of completeness and perfection because it is composed of the sacred numbers "3" (a sign of the superlative and the perfection of God's being and action) and "4" (a representation of cosmic totality). Christian tradition finds numerous uses for this number, including the seven angels before God's throne, the seven sacraments, the seven glories, joys, and sorrows of the Virgin Mary, and the seven virtues. Many legends associate the number with evil. For example, there are allegedly seven steps to hell. The Babylonians believed the seventh day (or any day that was a multiple of seven) to be a day of bad luck, and they felt it was dangerous to perform any important act on such a day. One variation that Poe might have had in mind when he penned "Shadow" speaks of the seven sleepers. Appearing world-wide in religious literature, this legend tells of the seven companions who fall asleep for centuries. Their sleep is frequently linked with disaster, sorrow, or seasonal change. This legend might have evolved out of the notion of falling asleep "in the Lord." Other stories by Poe feature this number. The revelers in "The Masque of the Red Death" occupy seven rooms, while in "The Pit and the Pendulum" the prisoner notices seven candles as he stands before the court. In "The Facts in the Case of M. Valdemar" the mesmerized man remains in this state for seven months. Later in "Hop-Frog," Poe's dwarf will enjoy "perfect" revenge when he destroys the King and his seven ministers. See Gertrude Jobes, *Dictionary of Mythology, Folklore, and Symbols* (New York: The Scarecrow Press, 1962), pp. 1421-1426.

11. Mabbott (Vol. 2, p. 188) states that the name Zoilus is connected with *zoë* meaning life. This idea establishes the connection between death and life.

12. For an interesting speculation on Poe's use of horror and humor in "Shadow" consult Fisher's *The Very Spirit of*

Cordiality, p. 10-11. See also Burton R. Pollin, "Poe's 'Shadow' as Prelude to 'The Masque of the Red Death,'" *Studies in Short Fiction* 6 (Fall 1968): 103-106.

13. See Joel Porte, *The Romance in America* (Middletown, Conn.: Wesleyan University Press, 1969), p. 55; and Edward H. Davidson, *Poe: A Critical Study* (Cambridge, Mass.: The Belknap Press of Harvard University Press, 1957), p. 5.

14. Benjamin Franklin Fisher IV, "The Power of Words in Poe's 'Silence,'" in his *Poe at Work*, p. 60.

15. Gerhard Hoffman, "Space and Symbol in the Tales of Edgar Allan Poe," *Poe Studies* 12 (June 1979): 2.

16. Hal Blythe and Charlie Sweet, "Poe's Satiric Use of Vampirism in 'Berenice,'" *Poe Studies* 14 (December 1981): 23-24.

17. Wilt, pp. 101-105.

18. See "Gothic Romanticism and Rational Empiricism in Poe's 'Berenice,'" p. 19.

19. John Ward Ostrom, ed., *The Letters of Edgar Allan Poe*, 2 vols. (New York: Gordian Press, 1966), Vol. 1, p. 57; and David E. E. Sloane and Benjamin Franklin Fisher IV, "Poe's Revisions in 'Berenice': Beyond the Gothic," *American Transcendental Quarterly* 24 (Fall 1974): 19-23.

20. Martin Bickman, "Animatopoeia: Morella as Siren of the Self," *Poe Studies* 8 (December 1975): 30. See also Bickman's remarks in *The Unsounded Centre: Jungian Studies in American Romanticism* (Chapel Hill: University of North Carolina Press, 1980), p. 68.

21. James W. Gargano, "Poe's 'Morella': A Note on Her Name," *American Literature* 47 (May 1975): 260.

22. Claudia Morrison, "Poe's 'Ligeia': An Analysis," *Studies in Short Fiction* 4 (Spring 1967): 244.

23. Michael Tritt, "'Ligeia' and 'The Conqueror Worm,'" *Poe Studies* 9 (June 1976): 22.

24. For an atypical transcendental perspective see Beverly Voloshin, "Transcendence Downward: An Essay on 'Usher' and 'Ligeia,'" *Modern Language Studies* 18 (Summer 1988): 18-29.

25. Consult Bruce Olson, "Poe's Strategy in 'The Fall of the House of Usher,'" *Modern Language Notes* 75 (November 1960): 556; Gerald M. Garmon, "Roderick Usher: Portrait of the Madman as Artist," *Poe Studies* 5 (June 1972): 11-14; E. Miller Budick, "The Fall of the House: A Reappraisal of Poe's Attitudes Toward Life and Death," *Southern Literary Journal* 9 (Spring 1977): 41; John L. Marsh, "The Psycho-Sexual Reading of 'The Fall of the House of Usher,'" *Poe Studies* 5 (June 1972): 8; Benjamin Franklin Fisher IV, "Poe's 'Usher' Tarred and Fethered," *Poe Studies* 6 (December 1973): 49; Walker, p. 49; and Renata R. Mautner Wasserman, "The Self, the Mirror, and the Other: 'The Fall of the House of Usher,'" *Poe Studies* 10 (December 1977): 33. Much recent critical opinion is synthesized in analyses by Patrick Quinn, G. R. Thompson, and Benjamin Franklin Fisher IV in *Ruined Eden of the Present--Hawthorne, Poe, and Melville: Critical Essays in Honor of Darrell Abel*, eds. G. R. Thompson and Virgil L. Lokke (West Lafayette, Ind.: Purdue University Press, 1981), pp. 303-374. These studies devolve from Abel's renowned "A Key to the House of Usher," *University of Toronto Quarterly* 18 (January 1949): 176-185. See also Lyle H. Kendall, "The Vampire Motif in 'The Fall of the House of Usher,'" *College English* 24 (March 1963): 50-53; J. O. Bailey, "What Happens in 'The Fall of the House of Usher'?," *American Literature* 35 (January 1964): 445-466; Howes, pp. 173-189; Ljungquist, *The Grand and the Fair*, pp. 100-106; and his "Howitt's 'Byronian Rambles' and the Picturesque Setting of 'The Fall of the House of Usher,'" *ESQ: A Journal of the American Renaissance* 33 (Number 4 1987): 224-236.

26. Wendy Stallard Flory, "Usher's Fear and the Flaw in Poe's Theories of the Metamorphosis of the Senses," *Poe Studies* 7 (June 1974): 19. See also Heller's *The Delights of Terror*, pp. 11, 127-146.

27. Robert Rogers, *A Psychoanalytic Study of the Double in*

Literature (Detroit: Wayne State University Press, 1970), p. 9.

28. Gerard M. Sweeney, "Beauty and Truth: Poe's 'A Descent into the Maelström,'" *Poe Studies* 6 (June 1973): 23. See also Fred Madden, "'A Descent into the Maelström': Suggestions of the Tall Tale," *Studies in the Humanities* 14 (December 1987): 127-138.

29. Rush, p. 325.

30. Consult Benjamin Franklin Fisher IV, "'Eleonora': Poe and Madness" in *Poe and His Times*, ed. B.F. Fisher IV, pp. 178-188; and Dayan, *Fables of the Mind*, pp. 210-223.

31. E. Arthur Robinson, "Cosmic Vision in Poe's 'Eleonora,'" *Poe Studies* 9 (December 1976): 44.

32. Rush, pp. 30, 325. See also Richard P. Benton, "'The Masque of the Red Death'--The Primary Source," *American Transcendental Quarterly* 1 (First Quarter, 1969): 12-13, in which the author speculates that Willis' description of a masked ball during a cholera epidemic provided Poe with the idea for this sketch. See also Pollin's "Poe's 'Shadow' as Prelude to 'The Masque of the Red Death.'"

33. Walter Blair, "Poe's Conception of Incident and Tone in the Tale," *Modern Philology* 41 (May 1944): 239.

34. David H. Hirsch, "The Pit and the Apocalypse," *Sewanee Review* 76 (Autumn 1968): 634.

35. James Lundquist, "The Moral of Averted Descent: The Failure of Sanity in 'The Pit and the Pendulum,'" *Poe Newsletter* 2 (April 1969): 26.

36. D.B. Tucker, "'The Tell-Tale Heart' and the 'Evil Eye,'" *Southern Literary Journal* 13 (Spring 1981): 95.

37. Rush, p. 153.

38. James W. Gargano, "'The Black Cat': Perverseness Reconsidered," *Texas Studies in Language and Literature* 2 (Summer 1960): 173.

39. Gayle Denington Anderson, "Demonology in 'The Black Cat,'" *Poe Studies* 10 (December 1977): 43.

40. Richard C. Frushell, "'An Incarnate Night-Mare': Moral Grotesquerie in 'The Black Cat,'" *Poe Studies* 5 (December 1972): 44.

41. J. Gerald Kennedy, "Poe and Magazine Writing on Premature Burial," *Studies in the American Renaissance* (1977): 165-178.

42. See Richard P. Benton, "Poe's 'The System of Dr. Tarr and Prof. Fether': Dickens or Willis?," *Poe Newsletter* 1 (April 1968): 7-9; and Benjamin Franklin Fisher IV, "Poe's 'Tarr and Fether': Hoaxing in the Blackwood Mode," in *The Naiad Voice: Essays on Poe's Satiric Hoaxing*, ed. Dennis W. Eddings (Port Washington: Associated Faculty Press, 1983), pp. 136-147.

43. Consult William Sumner Jenkins, *Pro-Slavery Thought in the Old South* (Chapel Hill: University of North Carolina Press, 1935), p. 29; and Louis Filler, *The Crusade Against Slavery* (New York: Harper and Brothers, 1960), pp. 14, 52, 92.

44. For example, see Ernest Marchand, "Poe as Social Critic," *American Literature* 6 (March 1934): 37; Bernard Rosenthal, "Poe, Slavery, and the *Southern Literary Messenger*: A Reexamination," *Poe Studies* 7 (December 1974): 29; Leslie Fiedler, *Love and Death in the American Novel* (New York: Dell, 1966), p. 377; Stuart Levine, "Poe and American Society," *The Canadian Review of American Studies* 9 (Spring 1978): 17; Bernard A. Drabeck, "'Tarr and Fether'--Poe and Abolitionism," *American Transcendental Quarterly* 14 (Spring 1972): 177; and Harry Levin, *The Power of Blackness: Hawthorne, Poe, Melville* (New York: Knopf, 1970), p. 121.

45. See Marchand, p. 37; and Rosenthal, pp. 29-38.

46. Burke, pp. 148-149.

47. See Kate Stewart,"The Supreme Madness: Revenge and the Bells in 'The Cask of Amontillado,'" *University of Mississippi Studies in English* n.s. 5 (1984-1987): 51-57.

48. For an interesting view of Poe's use of masquerades, see

James W. Gargano, *The Masquerade Vision in Poe's Short Stories* (Baltimore: The Edgar Allan Poe Society, 1977).

49. Charles A. Sweet, Jr., "Retapping Poe's 'Cask of Amontillado,'" *Poe Studies* 8 (June 1975): 10; "Montresor's Underlying Motive: Resampling 'The Cask of Amontillado,'" *University of Mississippi Studies in English* n.s. 6 (1988): 273-275.

50. Jay Jacoby, "Fortunato's Premature Demise in 'The Cask of Amontillado,'" *Poe Studies* 12 (December 1979): 31.

51. Drabeck believes that in "Hop-Frog" Poe issues a warning to slaveholders. See page 184.

Chapter 4

Poe's Fiction of Fear in Retrospect

A close reading of Poe's short stories allows us to see that he constructed his tales with a carefully calculated purpose in mind. Always the consummate craftsman, he adhered to a literary plan that would rely on the fears that haunted nineteenth-century readers. No liquor or laudanum produced the chilling scenes that appear in numerous Poe stories. Such episodes result from Poe's acutely astute sense of his audience's mental misgivings. The more closely we explore the depths of Poe's artistic creativity, the more clearly we recognize the genius of his imagination. We come to see that his artistic vision never blurred but remained, on the contrary, quite keen indeed.

An awareness of Benjamin Rush's *Diseases of the Mind* and Stephen King's *Danse Macabre* permits us to understand better Edgar Poe's strategy of fear. Fascinated by the various medical treatises that appeared during the early nineteenth century, Poe studied such works and used much of the knowledge imparted by these tomes in his own writing. *Diseases of the Mind* provided him with a theory concerning the human reaction to dread. In addition, Rush itemizes the particular fears that seemed most prevalent at the time. Determined to create an art form that embraced the doctrines of Gothic fiction, Poe used the ideas of the forerunner of modern American psychology to his own

127

advantage. King posits that the good horror writer must employ the "phobic pressure points" that exist in a particular society. The artist seeking aesthetic and financial success should be aware of his audience's psychic vulnerabilities. Horror triumphs only when it strikes its reader's secret chords of terror. Although he writes more than a hundred years after Poe's death, King discusses a theory of Gothic art that was no doubt present in Poe's mind. Conscious of the reservations residing deep in his reader's mental caverns, Poe attempts to bring these fears to the surface. He exploits both individual and societal misgivings. Since fear proves attractive, literature that incorporates this emotion virtually insures that it will achieve a devoted following who will easily fall prey to its magical influence. For Poe, then, the power of dread becomes vital to the overall impact of many of his literary creations.

At this point we should examine briefly Poe's tales of fear as they relate to his entire fictional canon. Versatile artist that he is, Poe does not restrict himself to the presentation of gruesome death, bizarre torture, or diseased thought. For years readers believed that Poe had been a drug- or alcohol-crazed madman who composed his sketches in the company of bats or ravens. Like beneficent wizards, numerous modern scholars have dispelled these mistaken notions. Terror is real, so Poe decided to present this sinister emotion as a hostile force that often assails human beings. His were not visions of dangerous fancy but images of reality. There are, however, less gloomy sides to his work. Poe's art, like a precious diamond, has many facets, all of which glisten enticingly. As Emily Dickinson would do later in the nineteenth century, Poe frequently viewed his subjects from different perspectives, and he seemed ready to admit that on occasion we must be willing to alter our approach to life. In recent years students of Poe have placed more emphasis on the humorous leanings of many of his pieces. Tales like "How to Write a Blackwood Article," "X-ing a Paragrab," and "Four Beasts in One/The Homo-Cameleopard" reveal that at times Poe could provoke his readers into fits of laughter. Ratiocinative stories such as "The Murders in the Rue Morgue" and "The Purloined Letter" celebrate the mind's positive abilities. Many of Poe's fear stories contain passages that appear somewhat "light." He realized that happiness and sorrow often walk hand in hand, and that ecstasy coexists with terror. The diverse nature of life manifests itself in the artistic efforts of Edgar Poe.

Yet Poe is perhaps best remembered for his tales of dread. The layman or scholar who hears Poe's name mentioned on the news or sees it in the local tabloid almost immediately recalls images of the crumbling home of Roderick Usher or the unnerving conclusion of "Ligeia." Perhaps this association results from the extreme intensity that Poe instills in his terror fiction. The power of these works reflects the strength of what may be the mightiest of human feelings--fear. We might wonder why Poe produced so many stories in which horror plays a central role. In all likelihood he wanted his audience to realize that in order to enjoy a healthy mental and physical life, all persons must face the specter of fear. If individuals react to this force in a manner similar to that of Roderick Usher, the speaker in "Silence," or Prince Prospero and his retinue, they will become its helpless victims. As Rush and King state, the mind must make a stand against this savage demon. Bravely facing this danger will lessen its impact. Poe's tales of terror attempt to use their readers' reservations to the author's advantage; this fact cannot be denied. They also hope to strengthen humanity's ability to endure fear's onslaught. Although man does not possess that capability to destroy completely this disturbing presence, he can mentally master it. Viewed in this light, Poe's fiction of fear does not oppress its readers with thoughts of fetid decay or death but instead emphasizes the ultimate value of life.

Selected Bibliography

Abel, Darrell. "A Key to the House of Usher." *University of Toronto Quarterly* 18 (January 1949): 176-185.

Anderson, Gayle Denington. "Demonology in 'The Black Cat.'" *Poe Studies* 10 (December 1977): 43-44.

Bailey, J. O. "What Happens in 'The Fall of the House of Usher'?" *American Literature* 35 (January 1964): 445-466.

Baym, Nina. "The Function of Poe's Pictorialism." *South Atlantic Quarterly* 65 (Winter 1966): 46-54.

Benton, Richard P. "Is Poe's 'The Assignation' a Hoax?" *Nineteenth-Century Fiction* 18 (September 1963): 193-197.

------. "'The Masque of the Red Death'--The Primary Source." *American Transcendental Quarterly* 1 (First Quarter 1969): 12-13.

------. "Poe's 'The System of Dr. Tarr and Prof. Fether': Dickens or Willis?" *Poe Newsletter* 1 (April 1968): 7-9.

Bickman, Martin. "Animatopoeia: Morella as Siren of the Self." *Poe Studies* 8 (December 1975): 30.

------. *The Unsounded Centre: Jungian Studies in American Romanticism.* Chapel Hill: University of North Carolina Press, 1980.

Binger, Carl. *Revolutionary Doctor: Benjamin Rush 1746-1813.* New York: Norton, 1966.

Birkhead, Edith. *The Tale of Terror.* New York: E.P. Dutton, 1920.

Blair, Walter. "Poe's Conception of Incident and Tone in the Tale." *Modern Philology* 41 (May 1944): 228-240.

Blythe, Hal, and Sweet, Charlie. "Poe's Satiric Use of Vampirism in 'Berenice.'" *Poe Studies* 14 (December 1981): 23-24.

Budick, E. Miller. "The Fall of the House: A Reappraisal of Poe's Attitudes Toward Life and Death." *Southern Literary Journal* 9 (Spring 1977): 30-50.

Burke, Edmund. *A Philosophical Enquiry into the Origin of Our Ideas of the Sublime and Beautiful*. London: R. & J. Dodsley, 1757; rpt., New York: Columbia University Press, 1958.

Butler, David W. "Usher's Hypochondriasis: Mental Alienation and Romantic Idealism in Poe's Gothic Tales." *American Literature* 48 (March 1976): 1-12.

Carlson, Eric W., ed. *The Recognition of Edgar Allan Poe: Selected Criticism Since 1829*. Ann Arbor: The University of Michigan Press, 1966.

Coad, Oral Sumner. "The Gothic Element in American Literature Before 1835." *Journal of English and Germanic Philology* 24 (January 1925): 72-93.

Conolly, John. *An Inquiry Concerning the Indications of Insanity*. London: John Taylor, 1830; rpt., London: Dawsons, 1964.

Cooke, P. Pendleton. "Edgar A. Poe." In *The Recognition of Edgar Allan Poe: Selected Criticism Since 1829*, pp. 21-28. Edited by Eric W. Carlson. Ann Arbor: The University of Michigan Press, 1966.

Dameron, J. Lasley. *Popular Literature: Poe's Not-so-soon Forgotten Lore*. Baltimore: The Edgar Allan Poe Society, 1980.

Davidson, Edward H. *Poe: A Critical Study*. Cambridge, Mass.: Belknap Press, 1957.

Davis, David B. *Homicide in American Fiction, 1798-1860: A Study in Social Values*. Ithaca: Cornell University Press, 1957.

Dayan, Joan. *Fables of Mind: An Inquiry into Poe's Fiction*. New York: Oxford University Press, 1987.

Defalco, Joseph M. "The Source of Terror in Poe's 'Shadow--A Parable.'" *Studies in Short Fiction* 6 (Fall 1969): 643-648.

Drabeck, Bernard A. "'Tarr and Fether'--Poe and Abolitionism."

American Transcendental Quarterly 14 (Spring 1972): 177-184.

Eddings, Dennis W., ed. *The Naiad Voice: Essays on Poe's Satiric Hoaxing.* Port Washington: Associated Faculty Press, 1983.

Eliot, T.S. "From Poe to Valery." In *The Recognition of Edgar Allan Poe: Selected Criticism Since 1829*, pp. 205-219. Edited by Eric W. Carlson. Ann Arbor: The University of Michigan Press, 1966.

Engel, Leonard W. "Identity and Enclosure in Edgar Allan Poe's 'William Wilson.'" *College Language Association Journal* 29 (September 1985): 91-99.

Errera, Paul. "Some Historical Aspects of the Concept of Phobia." *Psychiatric Quarterly* 36 (April 1962): 325-336.

Fagin, N. Bryllion. *The Histrionic Mr. Poe.* Baltimore: The Johns Hopkins Press, 1949.

Fiedler, Leslie. *Love and Death in the American Novel.* New York: Dell, 1966.

Filler, Louis. *The Crusade Against Slavery.* New York: Harper and Brothers, 1960.

Fisher, Benjamin Franklin, IV. "Blackwood Articles à la Poe: How to Make a False Start Play." *Revue Des Langues Vivantes* 39 (Winter 1973): 418-432.

------. "'Eleonora': Poe and Madness." In *Poe and His Times: The Artist and His Milieu*, pp. 178-188. Edited by B.F. Fisher IV. Baltimore: The Edgar Allan Poe Society, 1990.

------. "More Pieces in the Puzzle of Poe's 'The Assignation.'" In *Myths and Realities: The Mysterious Mr. Poe*, pp. 59-88. Edited by B. F. Fisher IV. Baltimore: The Edgar Allan Poe Society, 1987.

------, ed. *Myths and Reality: The Mysterious Mr. Poe.* Baltimore: The Edgar Allan Poe Society, 1987.

------. "Playful 'Germanism' in 'The Fall of the House of Usher.'" In *Ruined Eden of the Present--Hawthorne, Poe, and Melville: Critical Essays in Honor of Darell Abel*, pp. 355-374. Edited by G.R. Thompson and Virgil L. Locke. W. Lafayette, Ind.:

Purdue University Press, 1981.

------, ed. *Poe and His Times: The Artist and His Milieu.* Baltimore: The Edgar Allan Poe Society, 1990.

------. "Poe and the Art of the Well Wrought Tale." In *Poe at Work: Seven Textual Studies,* pp. 5-12. Edited by B.F. Fisher IV. Baltimore: The Edgar Allan Poe Society, 1978.

---------, ed. *Poe At Work: Seven Textual Studies.* Baltimore: The Edgar Allan Poe Society, 1978.

------. "Poe's 'Metzengerstein': Not a Hoax." *American Literature* 42 (January 1971): 487-494.

------. "Poe's 'Tarr and Fether': Hoaxing in the Blackwood Mode." In *The Naiad Voice: Essays on Poe's Satiric Hoaxing,* pp. 136-147. Edited by Dennis W. Eddings. Port Washington, NY: Associated Faculty Press, 1983.

------. "Poe's 'Usher' Tarred and Fethered." *Poe Studies* 6 (December 1973): 49.

------. "The Flights of a Good Man's Mind: Gothic Fantasy in Poe's 'The Assignation.'" *Modern Language Studies* 16 (Summer 1986): 27-34.

------. *The Gothic's Gothic: Study Aids to the Tradition of the Tale of Terror.* New York and London: Garland Publishing, Inc., 1988.

------. "The Power of Words in Poe's 'Silence.'" In *Poe at Work: Seven Textual Studies,* pp. 56-72. Edited by B.F. Fisher IV. Baltimore: The Edgar Allan Poe Society, 1978.

------. "The Residual Gothic Impulse: 1824-1873." In *Horror Literature: A Core Collection and Reference Guide,* pp. 176-220. Edited by Marshall B. Tymn. New York: R.R. Bowker, 1981.

------. *The Very Spirit of Cordiality: The Literary Uses of Alcohol and Alcoholism in the Tales of Edgar Allan Poe.* Baltimore: The Edgar Allan Poe Society, 1978.

------. "To 'The Assignation' from 'The Visionary' and Poe's Decade of Revising." *The Library Chronicle* 39 (Spring 1973): 89-105.

------. "To 'The Assignation' from 'The Visionary' (Part Two):

The Revisions and Related Matters." *The Library Chronicle* 40 (Winter 1976): 221-251.

Flory, Wendy Stallard. "Usher's Fear and the Flaw in Poe's Theories of the Metamorphosis of the Senses." *Poe Studies* 7 (June 1974): 17-19.

Foerster, Norman. *American Criticism.* Boston: Houghton-Mifflin, 1928.

Frushell, Richard C. "'An Incarnate Night-Mare': Moral Grotesquerie in 'The Black Cat.'" *Poe Studies* 5 (December 1972): 43-44.

Gargano, James W. "Poe's 'Morella': A Note on Her Name." *American Literature* 47 (May 1975): 259-264.

------. "'The Black Cat': Perverseness Reconsidered." *Texas Studies in Literature and Language* 2 (Summer 1960): 172-179.

------. *The Masquerade Vision in Poe's Short Stories.* Baltimore: The Edgar Allan Poe Society, 1977.

------. "The Question of Poe's Narrators." In *The Recognition of Edgar Allan Poe: Selected Criticism Since 1829*, pp. 308-316. Edited by Eric W. Carlson. Ann Arbor: The University of Michigan Press, 1966.

Garmon, Gerald M. "Roderick Usher: Portrait of the Madman as Artist." *Poe Studies* 5 (June 1972): 11-14.

Garrison, Joseph M., Jr. "The Function of Terror in the Work of Edgar Allan Poe." *American Quarterly* 18 (Summer 1966): 136-150.

Garner, Stanton. "Emerson, Thoreau, and Poe's 'Double Dupin,'" In *Poe and His Times: The Artist and His Milieu*, pp. 130-145. Edited by B.F. Fisher IV. Baltimore: The Edgar Allan Poe Society, 1990.

Gray, Jeffrey A. *The Psychology of Fear and Stress.* London: Weidenfeld and Nicolson, 1977.

Halio, Jay L. "The Moral Mr. Poe." *Poe Newsletter* 1 (October 1968): 23-24.

Hall, Calvin S., and Lindzey, Gardner. *Theories of Personality.* New York: John Wiley & Sons, 1970.

Hallie, Philip P. *The Paradox of Cruelty.* Middletown, Conn.: Wesleyan University Press, 1969.

Heller, Terry. "Poe's 'Ligeia' and the Pleasures of Terror." *Gothic* 2 (Spring 1980): 39-48.

------. *The Delights of Terror: An Aesthetics of the Tale of Terror.* Urbana, Ill.: University of Illinois Press, 1987.

Hemenway, Robert. "Gothic Sociology: Charles Chesnutt and the Gothic Mode." *Studies in the Literary Imagination* 7 (Spring 1974): 101-119.

Herndon, Jerry A. "Poe's 'Ligeia': Debts to Irving and Emerson," in *Poe and His Times: The Artist and His Milieu,* pp. 113-129. Edited by B.F. Fisher IV. Baltimore: The Edgar Allan Poe Society, 1990.

Hirsch, David H. "Poe's 'Metzengerstein' as a Tale of the Subconscious." *University of Mississippi Studies in English* n.s. 3 (1982): 40-52.

------. "The Pit and the Apocalypse." *Sewanee Review* 76 (Autumn 1968): 632-652.

Hoffman, Gerhard. "Space and Symbol in the Tales of Edgar Allan Poe." *Poe Studies* 12 (June 1979): 1-14.

Howes, Craig. "Burke, Poe, and 'Usher': The Sublime and Rising Woman." *ESQ: A Journal of the American Renaissance* 13 (Third Quarter 1985): 173-189.

Hume, Robert. "Gothic vs. Romantic: A Revaluation of the Gothic Novel." *PMLA* 84 (March 1969): 282-290.

Hungerford, Edward. "Poe and Phrenology." *American Literature* 2 (November 1930): 209-231.

Hutcherson, Dudley R. "Poe's Reputation in England and America, 1850-1909." *American Literature* 14 (November 1942): 211-233.

Jackson, David K. *Poe and the Southern Literary Messenger.* Richmond: Dietz Printing Company, 1934.

Jacobs, Robert D. *Poe: Journalist and Critic.* Baton Rouge: Louisiana State University Press, 1969.

Jacoby, Jay. "Fortunato's Premature Demise in 'The Cask of Amontillado.'" *Poe Studies* 12 (December 1979): 30-31.

Jenkins, William Sumner. *Pro-Slavery Thought in the Old South.* Chapel Hill: University of North Carolina Press, 1935.

Jobes, Gertrude. *Dictionary of Mythology, Folklore, and Symbols.* New York: The Scarecrow Press, 1962.

Keech, James M. "The Survival of the Gothic Response." *Studies in the Novel* 6 (Summer 1974): 130-145.

Kendall, Lyle H. "The Vampire Motif in 'The Fall of the House of Usher.'" *College English* 24 (March 1963): 50-53.

Kendrick, Walter. *The Thrill of Fear: 250 Years of Scary Entertainment.* New York: Grove Weidenfeld, 1991.

Kennedy, J. Gerald. "Poe and Magazine Writing on Premature Burial." *Studies in the American Renaissance* (1977): 165-178.

------. *Poe, Death, and the Life of Writing.* New Haven: Yale University Press, 1987.

Ketterer, David. "The Sexual Abyss: Consummation in 'The Assignation.'" *Poe Studies* 19 (June 1986): 7-10.

King, Stephen. *Danse Macabre.* New York: Everest House, 1981.

Laverty, Carroll. "Science and Pseudo-Science in the Writings of Edgar Allan Poe." Ph.D. dissertation, Duke University, 1951.

Lawrence, D. H. "Edgar Allan Poe." In *The Recognition of Edgar Allan Poe: Selected Criticism Since 1829*, pp. 110-126. Edited by Eric W. Carlson. Ann Arbor: The University of Michigan Press, 1966.

Levin, Harry. *The Power of Blackness: Hawthorne, Poe, Melville.* New York: Knopf, 1970.

Levine, Stuart. "Poe and American Society." *The Canadian Review of American Studies* 9 (Spring 1978): 16-33.

Lewis, Paul. "Laughing at Fear: Two Versions of the Mock Gothic." *Studies in Short Fiction* 15 (Fall 1978): 411-414.

Ljungquist, Kent. "Burke's *Enquiry* and the Aesthetics of 'The Pit and the Pendulum.'" *Poe Studies* 11 (December 1978): 26-29.

------. "Howitt's 'Byronian Rambles' and the Picturesque Setting of 'The Fall of the House of Usher.'" *ESQ: A Journal of the American Renaissance* 33 (Number 4 1987): 224-236.

------. *The Grand and the Fair: Poe's Landscape Aesthetics and Pictorial Techniques*. Potomoc, Md.: Scripta Humanistica, 1984.

Lovecraft, H.P. *Supernatural Horror in Literature*. New York: B. Abramson, 1945; rpt., New York: Dover, 1973.

Lundblad, Jane. *Nathaniel Hawthorne and the European Literary Tradition*. Upsala: Almquist & Wiksells, 1946; rpt., New York: Russell and Russell, 1965.

Lundquist, James. "The Moral of Averted Descent: The Failure of Sanity in 'The Pit and the Pendulum.'" *Poe Newsletter* 2 (April 1969): 25-26.

Madden, Fred. "'A Descent into the Maelström': Suggestions of the Tall Tale." *Studies in the Humanities* 14 (1987): 127-138.

Marchand, Ernest. "Poe as Social Critic." *American Literature* 6 (March 1934): 28-43.

Marks, Isaac M. *Fears and Phobias*. New York: Academic Press, 1969.

Marsh, John L. "The Psycho-Sexual Reading of 'The Fall of the House of Usher.'" *Poe Studies* 5 (June 1972): 8-9.

Morrison, Claudia. "Poe's 'Ligeia': An Analysis." *Studies in Short Fiction* 4 (Spring 1967): 234-244.

Moss, Sidney P. *Poe's Literary Battles*. Durham: Duke University Press, 1963.

Mussell, Kay. "Gothic Novels." In *Handbook of American Popular Culture*, pp. 151-169. Edited by M. Thomas Inge. Westport, Conn.: Greenwood Press, 1978.

Nelson, Lowry, Jr. "Night Thoughts on the Gothic Novel." *Yale Review* 52 (December 1962): 236-257.

Obuchowski, Peter. "Unity of Effect in Poe's 'The Fall of the House of Usher.'" *Studies in Short Fiction* 12 (Fall 1975): 407-412.

Olson, Bruce. "Poe's Strategy in 'The Fall of the House of Usher.'" *Modern Language Notes* 75 (November 1960): 556-559.

Ostrom, John Ward. *The Letters of Edgar Allan Poe*. 2 vols. Cambridge, Mass.: Harvard University Press, 1948; rpt., New

York: Gordian Press, 1966.

Otto, Rudolph. *The Idea of the Holy: An Inquiry into the Non-rational Factor in the Idea of the Divine and Its Relation to the Rational*. Translated by John Harvey. London: Oxford University Press, 1952.

Pahl, Dennis. *Architects of the Abyss: The Indeterminate Fictions of Poe, Hawthorne, and Melville*. Columbia: University of Missouri Press, 1989.

------. "Recovering Byron: Poe's 'The Assignation.'" *Criticism* 26 (Spring 1984): 111-119.

Parrington, Vernon Lewis. *The Romantic Revolution in America, 1800-1860*. New York: Harcourt, Brace, 1927.

Pattee, Fred Lewis. *The Development of the American Short Story*. New York: Harper and Brothers, 1923; rpt., New York: Biblo and Tannen, 1966.

Phillips, Elizabeth. *Edgar Allan Poe: An American Imagination*. Port Washington: Kennikat Press, 1979.

Poe, Edgar Allan. *Collected Works of Edgar Allan Poe*. Edited by Thomas Ollive Mabbott. Cambridge, Mass.: Belknap Press, 1978.

------. *Marginalia*. Introduction by John Carl Miller. Charlottesville: University Press of Virginia, 1981.

------. *The Complete Works of Edgar Allan Poe*. Edited by James A. Harrison. New York: Thomas Y. Crowell, 1902; rpt., New York: AMS Press, 1965.

Pollin, Burton R., ed. *Collected Writings of Edgar Allan Poe*: Volume 2, *The Brevities*. New York: Gordian Press, 1985.

------. "Poe 'Viewed and *Reviewed*': An Annotated Checklist of Contemporaneous Notices." *Poe Studies* 13 (December 1980): 17-28.

------. "Poe's 'Shadow' as Prelude to 'The Masque of the Red Death.'" *Studies in Short Fiction* 6 (Fall 1968): 103-106.

Porte, Joel. *The Romance in America*. Middletown, Conn.: Wesleyan University Press, 1969.

Punter, David. *The Literature of Terror: A History of Gothic Fiction from 1765 to the Present Day*. New York: Longman,

1980.

Quinn, Arthur Hobson. *Edgar Allan Poe: A Critical Biography.* New York: Appleton-Century-Crofts, 1941.

Rachman, Stanley. *The Meanings of Fear.* Baltimore: Penguin, 1974.

------. *Phobias: Their Nature and Control.* Springfield, Ill.: Charles C. Thomas, 1968.

Redden, Mary Maurita. *The Gothic Fiction in the American Magazines (1765-1800).* Washington, D.C.: Catholic University of America Press, 1939.

Ridgely, J.V. "George Lippard's *The Quaker City*: The World of the American Porno-Gothic." *Studies in the Literary Imagination* 7 (Spring 1974): .77-94.

Robertson, Patricia. "Poe's 'The Cask of Amontillado'-- Again." *Publications of the Arkansas Philological Society* 14 (1988): 39-46.

Robinson, E. Arthur. "Cosmic Vision in Poe's 'Eleonora.'" *Poe Studies* 9 (December 1976): 44-46.

Rogers, Robert. *A Psychoanalytic Study of the Double in Literature.* Detroit: Wayne State University Press, 1970.

Rosenthal, Bernard. "Poe, Slavery, and the *Southern Literary Messenger*: A Reexamination." *Poe Studies* 7 (December 1974): 29-38.

Rubin, Louis D., Jr. "The Other Side of Slavery: Thomas Nelson Page's 'No Haid Pawn.'" *Studies in the Literary Imagination* 7 (Spring 1974): 95-99.

Rush, Benjamin. *Medical Inquiries and Observations upon the Diseases of the Mind.* Philadelphia: Kimber and Richardson, 1812.

Russ, Joanna. "Somebody's Trying to Kill Me and I Think It's My Husband: The Modern Gothic." *Journal of Popular Culture* 6 (Spring 1973): 666-691.

St. Armand, Barton Levi. "The 'Mysteries' of Edgar Poe: The Quest for the Monomyth in Gothic Literature." In *The Gothic Imagination: Essays in Dark Romanticism*, pp. 65-93. Edited by G.R. Thompson. Pullman: Washington State

University Press, 1974.

------. *The Roots of Horror in the Fiction of H.P. Lovecraft*. New York: Dragon Press, 1977.

Saliba, David R. *A Psychology of Fear: The Nightmare Formula of Edgar Allan Poe*. Lanham, Md.: University Press of America, 1980.

Sedgwick, Eve Kosofsky. "The Character in the Veil: Imagery of the Surface in the Gothic Novel." *PMLA* 96 (March 1981): 255-270.

Shelden, Pamela J. "'True Originality': Poe's Manipulation of the Gothic Tradition." *American Transcendental Quarterly* 29 (Winter 1976): 75-80.

Shulman, Robert. "Poe and the Powers of the Mind." *ELH* 37 (June 1970): 245-262.

Silverman, Kenneth. *Edgar A. Poe: Mournful and Never-ending Remembrance*. New York: Harper Collins, 1991.

Sloane, David E.E. "Early Nineteenth-Century Medicine in Poe's Short Stories." M.A. thesis, Duke University, 1966.

------. "Gothic Romanticism and Rational Empiricism in Poe's 'Berenice.'" *American Transcendental Quarterly* 19 (Summer 1973): 19-26.

------, and Fisher, Benjamin Franklin, IV. "Poe's Revisions in 'Berenice': Beyond the Gothic." *American Transcendental Quarterly* 24 (Fall 1974): 19-23.

------. "Usher's Nervous Fever: The Meaning of Medicine in Poe's 'The Fall of the House of Usher.'" In *Poe and His Times: The Artist and His Milieu*, pp. 146-153. Edited by B.F. Fisher IV. Baltimore: The Edgar Allan Poe Society, 1990.

Soule, George H. "Byronism in Poe's 'Metzengerstein' and 'William Wilson.'" *ESQ: A Journal of the American Renaissance* 24 (Third Quarter 1978): 152-162.

Stauffer, Donald Barlow. "The Two Styles of Poe's 'MS. Found in a Bottle.'" *Style* 1 (Spring 1967): 107-120.

Stewart, Kate. "The Supreme Madness: Revenge and the Bells in 'The Cask of Amontillado.'" *University of Mississippi Studies in English* n.s. 5 (1984-1987): 51-57.

Stoehr, Taylor. "'Unspeakable Horror' in Poe." *South Atlantic Quarterly* 78 (Summer 1979): 317-332.

Summers, Montague. *The Gothic Quest.* London: Fortune Press, 1938; rpt., New York: Russell & Russell, 1964.

Sweeney, Gerard M. "Beauty and Truth: Poe's 'A Descent into the Maelström.'" *Poe Studies* 6 (June 1973): 22-25.

Sweet, Charles A., Jr. "Montresor's Underlying Motive: Resampling 'The Cask of Amontillado.'" *University of Mississippi Studies in English* n.s. 6 (1988): 273-275.

------. "Retapping Poe's 'Cask of Amontillado.'" *Poe Studies* 8 (June 1975): 10-12.

Thompson, G. R. *Poe's Fiction: Romantic Irony in the Gothic Tales.* Madison: University of Wisconsin Press, 1973.

------, ed. *Romantic Gothic Tales: 1790-1840.* New York: Harper & Row, 1979.

------, ed. *The Gothic Imagination: Essays in Dark Romanticism.* Pullman: Washington State University Press, 1974.

------, and Locke, Virgil L., eds. *Ruined Eden of the Present-- Hawthorne, Poe, and Melville: Critical Essays in Honor of Darell Abel.* West Lafayette, Ind.: Purdue University Press, 1981.

Thompson, Stith. *Motif-Index of Folk-Literature.* Bloomington, Ind.: Indiana University Press, 1955-1958.

Todorov, Tzvetan. *The Fantastic: A Structural Approach to a Literary Genre.* Translated by Richard Howard. Cleveland: The Press of Case Western Reserve University, 1973.

Tritt, Michael. "'Ligeia' and 'The Conqueror Worm.'" *Poe Studies* 9 (June 1976): 21-22.

Tucker, D.B. "'The Tell-Tale Heart' and the 'Evil Eye.'" *Southern Literary Journal* 13 (Spring 1981): 92-98.

Tupper, Martin Farquhar. "American Romance." In *The Recognition of Edgar Allan Poe: Selected Criticism Since 1829*, pp. 18-21. Edited by Eric W. Carlson. Ann Arbor: The University of Michigan Press, 1966.

Tymn, Marshall B., ed. *Horror Literature: A Core Collection and Reference Guide.* New York: R. R. Bowker, 1981.

Varma, Devendra P. *The Gothic Flame*. London: Arthur Barker Ltd., 1957.

Voloshin, Beverly. "Transcendence Downward: An Essay on 'Usher' and 'Ligeia.'" *Modern Language Studies* 18 (Summer 1988): 18-29.

Voss, Arthur. *The American Short Story: A Critical Survey*. Norman: University of Oklahoma Press, 1973.

Walker, I.M. "The 'Legitimate Sources' of Terror in 'The Fall of the House of Usher.'" *Modern Language Review* 61 (October 1966): 585-592.

Wasserman, Renata R. Mautner. "The Self, the Mirror, and the Other: 'The Fall of the House of Usher.'" *Poe Studies* 10 (December 1977): 33-35.

Whisnant, David E. "Edgar Allan Poe's Study of Science." M.A. thesis, Duke University, 1962.

Wilbur, Richard. "The House of Poe." In *The Recognition of Edgar Allan Poe: Selected Criticism Since 1829*, pp. 245-277. Edited by Eric W. Carlson. Ann Arbor: The University of Michigan Press, 1966.

Wilson, James D. "Incest and American Romantic Fiction." *Studies in the Literary Imagination* 7 (Spring 1974): 31-50.

Wilt, Napier. "Poe's Attitude Toward His Tales: A New Document." *Modern Philology* 25 (August 1927): 101-105.

Zanger, Jules. "Poe and the Theme of Forbidden Knowledge." *American Literature* 49 (January 1978): 533-543.

Index